for the Love of Birds

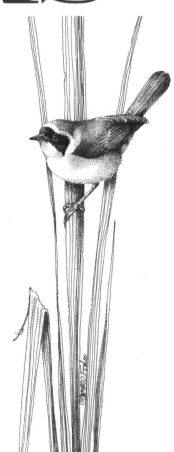

by Kay Charter

illustrations by
Thomas W. Ford

Crofton Creek Press
South Boardman, Michigan

First Edition

10 9 8 7 6 5 4 3 2 1

Published by Crofton Creek Press
2303 Gregg Road SW, South Boardman, MI 49680
www.croftoncreek.com

This edition of *For the Love of Birds* was printed by Jostens, State
College, Pennsylvania. The book was designed and composed by
D. Warren Truax. It is set in Slimbach Book, a typeface designed for
digital composition by Robert Slimbach based on the eighteenth-century
typefaces of Hermann Zapf. This book is printed on acid-free paper
and Smyth sewn for maximum durability.

Library of Congress Cataloging-in-Publication Data

Charter, Kay, 1939-
     For the love of birds / by Kay Charter ; illustrations by Thomas W.
Ford.-- 1st ed.
         p. cm.
     Includes bibliographical references (p.   ).
     ISBN 0-9700917-1-0 (alk. paper)
     1. Birds--Anecdotes. 2. Charter, Kay, 1939-   . I. Title.
QL673 .C446 2000
598--dc21
                                                        00-012011

Contents

Dedicated to Dr. Bob

1

SANCTUARY

Twenty years ago, no one could have persuaded me that one day birds would be the center of my life. Back then, all ducks were mallards, the only songbird I could identify was the American robin, and I accepted my grandfather's pronouncement that sparrows should be shot.

But I discovered the pleasure of watching birds shortly before my husband, Jimmy, and I quit our jobs in San Diego and sold our home in order to tour North America. As we criss-crossed the continent from the Yukon to Florida and from Nova Scotia back to San Diego, birding became more important and we began to seek out new species to add to our life lists. We took a boat out of Homer, Alaska, in search of puffins, drove to the end of the Keys to find magnificent frigatebirds, and hiked across Quebec's Bonaventure Island to watch a colony of nesting gannets.

Our journey eventually brought us to northern Michigan

where we ultimately sank virtually all of our worldly assets into forty-seven acres of land for the sole purpose of aiding migrating and nesting songbirds. Along the way, we've given up any financial security we might have had, watched our possessions go up in smoke, and suffered a serious trauma. In spite of our setbacks, we wouldn't trade places with anyone. The rewards and challenges of acting as stewards for the birds on this land, which we call Charter Sanctuary, have exceeded our greatest hopes and our highest expectations.

When we first arrived on the tip of the Leelanau Peninsula, we bought a Victorian house in Jimmy's hometown of Northport and turned it into a bed-and-breakfast inn. Three years later, we sold the old house and built a cottage in the center of a densely wooded lot on the shores of Lake Michigan's Grand Traverse Bay.

Until we built our home on the water, my interest in birds, though both serious and satisfying, had not developed into a consuming passion. But not long after we moved in, a single mite of a bird showed up outside our window and stole my heart. It was mid-May—the height of spring migration. One morning I was painting window trim in a second-floor bedroom when a morsel of fiery orange flashed through a cedar on the other side of the glass. It was a bird with a brilliant orange throat and face. He had black ear patches, a finely streaked pale yellow belly, and his black wings and back wore splashes of pure white. Though I had never seen him before, I immediately recognized him from pictures in our field guides. It was a male Blackburnian warbler.

I stopped painting to watch him poke around the flat, dense sprays of cedar leaves. He worked his way quickly through the branches and then moved to the next tree north. Then I realized he was not alone. The trees were filled with other colorful little warblers. Nashville, chestnut-sided, and magnolia warblers foraged through the dense branches alongside their striking relative. A single American redstart moved among them. The birds fed quickly, and then leapfrogged past each other in their collective northward journey.

The scope and wonder of spring migration was new to

me. Jimmy and I already considered ourselves conservationists. We belonged to organizations like the National Wildlife
Federation, the Nature Conservancy, and the National Audubon
Society. We incorporated used materials in our home, built it
with six-inch walls to reduce heat loss, and recycled every can,
jar, box, and scrap of paper that came into the house. But watching the brilliant Blackburnian and his colorful cousins raised
my awareness of how critical this highway of trees was during
migration. It brought me face to face with the need to protect
and preserve as much habitat as possible for these marvelous
migrants, and that meant more than just hauling Coke cans
back to the grocer.

During the building process, we left as much of the natural surroundings as we could, but construction necessarily de-
stroys some of the environment. The wealth of birds around
us, especially the warblers, inspired us to do more on their
behalf once our home was finished. After we moved in, we
replaced trees and shrubs that had been removed during con-

struction. We also developed a hummingbird garden, created brush piles, and constructed a pond for our avian visitors.

Two summers later, I was sitting on a boulder working at the edge of our driveway when a pair of tiny brown birds with short, stiff tails angling up over their rumps popped out from a hollow under the roots of a nearby downed tree. The pair chattered and fussed as they moved among the roots. In a moment, another little bird—a plump carbon copy of the first two—ventured out to join them. Another followed, and another, and after a brief pause, a fourth little bird crept out from under the hollow.

This was a nest of fledgling winter wrens making their collective debut on the earth's grand stage, a sight seldom seen by humans. I sat stone still so as not to alarm them, then watched in awe as the parents coaxed their young away from the protective roots that had served as their nursery. For long minutes the wren family scrambled across the leaf litter of the forest floor, parents hunting for insects and youngsters begging for food. Then they scurried off in search of richer foraging grounds.

After they were gone, I thought about the damp, coniferous woods required by these tiny birds, whose complex flute-like melodies—sweet and pure as a Mozart minuet—fill wet woodlands in the spring. And I was struck with the realization that that kind of habitat was falling increasingly to development here in northern Michigan.

If the Blackburnian warbler stole my heart, the wren family transformed my life. The intense pleasure at being present for the scene I had just witnessed dissolved into an almost overwhelming sadness at the thought that these fascinating songbirds might some day vanish from our increasingly manicured environment.

My distress generated an idea that I took to Jimmy. The value of our lakefront property had skyrocketed since we built our cottage. If we sold our beachside home on its half-acre lot, we could take the profit and buy a much larger parcel away from the water where we could establish a sanctuary for migrating and nesting songbirds like warblers and winter wrens.

In the thirty years of our relationship, I have never known my steady, low-key mate to jump at anything. His youngest daughter says that "Dad forever said 'maybe' to every request when we were growing up. But we all knew that 'maybe' meant 'yes.'" If maybe meant yes, then the emphatic yes he gave to this proposal amounted to raving support.

A few short months later, the home on the water belonged to someone else, and we had adequate funds to buy our land. We began our search immediately. Any undeveloped tract would have served as a refuge for some species, but in order to attract and aid the largest numbers and widest variety, we needed a mixture of habitats. Wetlands—one of the most productive habitats on the planet—were essential. A woods was desirable and so was upland meadow. Finding all three in something we could afford would be a step into heaven.

After we sold the house on the bay, we moved back temporarily into the Victorian house in Northport where we'd had our B&B. The new owners, Carl and Mary Lou Griffin, whom we met when they came as guests, had purchased it for a summer place. They had become good friends and generously loaned it to us while we looked for land.

That autumn we rejected several places and tried unsuccessfully to purchase two others. Fall gave way to winter and we began to prepare for our annual birding trek to Texas. A week before our scheduled departure, we learned of a tract just outside the nearby village of Omena.

We had driven past the property many times and knew its perimeter well. But we'd never seen the interior. It was December when we set out to look at it—during a driving snowstorm on the coldest day of the year. As we trudged to the top of the hill on the eastern boundary, snow spilled into our boots and the wind stung our faces. But as soon as we reached the top, the bitter cold and driving snow were forgotten. It was exactly what we were looking for.

Below us lay a quarter mile of creek that ran first through a wet woodland before spreading into a broad cattail pond surrounded by native willows and red osier dogwood. Staghorn sumac thriving on the hillside below us was bordered by pin cherries, serviceberries, and other native pioneer species. A narrow belt of hardwood forest lined the southern edge of the property and several small stands of white pine were sprinkled among the pin cherries. Across the creek, opposite the hill where we stood, was a rolling, upland meadow.

All or any part of the forty-seven acres was available for a given amount per acre. I asked Jimmy if he thought we could stretch our budget for at least twenty acres, which would give us the hillside, the creek, and some of the meadow.

He thought for a long time before answering.

"We should buy all of it," he said finally.

Buying the entire piece would leave us with barely enough to build a home and nothing for the modest nest egg we had planned. I didn't see how we could justify spending that much and said so.

"I think you'll be sorry if we don't buy all of it," he said.

Two months later we owned the entire forty-seven acres—woodland, wetland, hillside, and meadow. As soon as winter released its snowy grip on Leelanau County, we selected our building site overlooking the cattails, and then built a three-car detached garage that would provide storage for our possessions while we built our home. We called it a "barn" to differentiate it from the garage that would be attached to the house. After our house was done, our barn would provide shelter for the old Ford tractor, Jimmy's vast collection of building tools, and his growing collection of gardening equipment. That year when we left for Texas, the barn was finished and filled with virtually all of our belongings. We had also completed the shell for the house, including roof, windows, doors, and subfloor.

We returned on April 12, unpacked the car, and went straight to check on our property and buildings. Everything was just as we had left it.

When we went to bed that night, a thunderstorm raged outside. The phone rang in the middle of the night; Jimmy's brother, Fred, who was fire chief in our town, was on the other end. The conversation was short. Lightening had struck our barn.

"Maybe it was the house," Jimmy said hopefully when he

hung up. We hoped so. Oh, how we hoped that was so. The house, after all, only held his table saw, a compressor, and a few hand tools.

We dressed and drove out to our place to find that Fred's report had been right. The fire department was there but it was too late for fire fighting. By the time someone saw the blaze and called it in, all that was left of the twenty-by-thirty-foot structure and its contents were the twisted remains of two metal overhead doors. Our furniture, most of our clothing, a few objects of art, an eclectic collection of kitchen goods, and a lifetime of family photos and letters—including correspondence from my beloved friend Max, written during the time he fought an ultimately fatal illness—as well as other memorabilia and treasures had gone up in smoke. My grandmother's china was gone. So was Jimmy's family Bible.

Having to rebuild the barn and replace our things set our plans back a year. Habitat improvements and the class I'd hoped to teach would have to wait at least until the following spring.

Losing all our possessions in a fire was painful, but it wasn't, as some suggested, a tragedy. No lives were lost...no one was even hurt. And the habitat remained untouched. That was a tremendous blessing in the middle of our unfortunate experience. If the trees had burned, we would never have lived long enough to see them grow back. We've been told that one particular gnarly river birch growing alongside our creek is over a hundred years old.

With the help of family and friends (and an insurance company with an incredible heart), we rebuilt the barn, finished our house, and replaced our lost possessions. A week before Christmas we moved into our new home.

But lady bad luck wasn't through with us. Two years later, Jimmy fell off the back of our motor home and broke his back.

When we spent more than we had intended on our land, we first tried to make up the difference by selling our individual skills. I worked to move my writing beyond my local birding column into more lucrative markets, and Jimmy was a carpenter for hire. His skills were excellent and more easily promoted than mine. Before our house was even finished, we

had a list of locals waiting for a variety of repairs and remodels on their respective homes. After his fall, however, that income vanished.

The accident happened in Tucson. Light drizzle covered the ladder steps on the back of our motor home with just enough moisture to make them slippery. Jimmy was descending the ladder and halfway down his feet slid out from under him. He fell six feet to the ground, landing on his tailbone and left hand. The third vertebra up from the base of his spine was shattered. So was his wrist. The damage was repaired by an excellent young orthopedic surgeon, Rolando Roberto. After the surgery Jimmy was ultimately able to walk and do most of what he did before. But there were permanent limitations. Among them was the fact that he couldn't lift more than twenty pounds without a painful payback. Moving his table saw and heavy construction materials was out of the question. That meant no more of the remodeling work that had been his bread and butter.

My career began to move forward, but it didn't bring in enough to fill the financial gap. We had discussed selling off a portion of the property when we first bought it, but when our financial squeeze set in, we never considered the possibility of actually parting with any of it—even though the value of property in our county is so high that selling a single lot would have entirely resolved our personal economic problems. But giving up any piece would have meant sacrificing nest habitat for one or more species, and we simply could not do that. Instead, we turned again to the business we thought we'd left behind forever, even though we had to give up our own bed in order to do it. We opened our home as a bed-and-breakfast inn. Then I went to work—first in a gift shop and then at a nearby inn where I made beds, schlepped laundry, and cleaned toilets.

All for the love of birds.

2

PLEASANT SURPRISES

My husband and I are not experts. When we bought this land we were not certain which species were suffering the greatest losses, which might be attracted to our sanctuary to nest, and how many species would visit this land to feed or rest during migration. But we did know that habitat destruction is responsible for most population declines, and we simply set out to provide the most varied habitat possible.

The result has surprised us. It has also surprised some experts. My son, Jeff, is a professional birder, and after spending a summer here he commented that he'd never visited such a "birdy" place in such a relatively small space—at least not in North America.

In the seven short years that we have owned this land, we have hosted at least fifty-two species of nesting birds. Forty are songbirds; five of those are warblers. Black-billed cuckoos have nested here. Rose-breasted grosbeaks, indigo buntings, and

Baltimore orioles are regulars. We have seen a hundred additional species on our sanctuary. Some, like the upland sandpiper that showed up with a chick alongside our driveway recently, come to forage after nesting. But we have seen most of the non-nesting species during migration.

The breeding bird census for our land is probably low. Because our trail system is incomplete, and because we do not go off our trails for fear of disturbing ground nesters, there are many parts of our land that we don't see during the breeding season, and those areas undoubtedly host nesting birds. We don't seek out nests to count them because we fear attracting predators to them. We document as nesters only those birds we see engaging in breeding, nesting, or feeding behavior within the boundaries of our land.

Not only were we surprised by the number of birds the land hosted, we were amazed by the incredible bird activity we've been able to watch from inside our home. When we built the house, we positioned it against a row of wild pin cherries that runs along the edge of a wetland that can be seen from our living room's bay window. That bay window turned out to be the best bird-watching spot on the entire property. We have observed phoebes feeding fledglings in the pin cherries that were so close to the window we could easily have touched them. In the fall, ruffed grouse pluck grapes from vines climbing up the trees, woodcock poke for worms in the soft earth underneath, and, one afternoon in late summer, I walked into the room to find myself eyeball-to-eyeball with a Cooper's hawk.

When we sold our place on the bay, I feared we would no longer be able to watch the colorful spring spectacle of abundant songbirds working their way northward through our cedar-hemlock woods. My concern was unfounded; our wetland and creek are part of an equally rich wildlife corridor. Rather than missing the grand avian parade on its way north, we have actually seen more species on this land than we did before, and we have watched them in far greater numbers. One year during the height of spring migration, I counted thirteen warbler species in a single hour outside that bay window.

We have been delighted with our successes; both the

number of species and the number of individuals nesting here have increased since we came. That is the result of habitat improvements. We have made a few of those improvements by planting hundreds of pine, hemlock, and cedar saplings and by mounting nest ledges and boxes. But Mother Nature carried out most of the habitat work without our help. There were no upland nesters during our first year; now there are many pairs of half a dozen species. Our wetland was half pond when we came, but the natural silting process has turned it into a dense tangle of cattails, horsetail, and willows. The hillside, with its emergent pioneer plants, is growing up at an unbelievable rate, and the woodland along the creek on the north is spreading beyond its borders.

As the woodlands expand and mature, we may eventually host others, like the Blackburnian warblers and winter wrens that were so important to my interest in birds. While both species currently occur during migration, neither nests here—at least not yet. Providing for them is one of our goals.

3

AT PLAY IN THE FIELD
WITH SWALLOWS

People often ask me which bird is my favorite, and my response is a little like that of a woman with a large family when asked to name her favorite child. Depending on the day, it could be one of many. When the bobolinks return to our meadows from their wintering grounds in the Argentine grasslands, I always say without question that this is my favorite species. I can't resist a male bobolink's glorious song as he defends his harem from other bobolinks.

If asked my favorite when the Blackburnian warbler—the bird noted avian authority Kenn Kaufman calls the "fiery gem of the treetops"—is foraging through our woodlands en route to its breeding grounds, this brilliant little bird tops my list. And it goes without saying that the black-capped chickadee, one of which insists on following me around our property and begging for seed from my pocket, is a perennial favorite.

Then there is the tree swallow. This small and beautiful

songbird has a white breast and belly and iridescent blue-green back. Its rather short, plump body and the fact that is has virtually no neck give it the appearance of a tiny winged torpedo. Like all swallows, it feeds on insects in flight and is necessarily an agile aerialist capable of quick turns, sudden dives, and steep climbs. Tree swallows on the wing remind me of fighter jets under the skillful hands of highly trained pilots. They are the "Top Guns" of the bird world. They are wonderful to watch and listen to as they sing their bubbling melodies while swooping and gliding over open fields and upland meadows.

Tree swallows are cavity nesters that once settled in the cavities of dead or dying trees to raise their broods. But as such trees increasingly fell under chainsaw and ax, these birds were forced to look elsewhere for suitable nest sites. They still use natural cavities where they are available, but many now use the man-made boxes that are usually put up to attract bluebirds. This phenomenon has allowed thousands of people like Jimmy and me to watch tree swallow courtship and nesting at close range. Every year we have added nest boxes around the property as increasing numbers of swallows arrive looking for homes.

One spring we received a package from Jeff's bird-loving fiancée, Becky. Inside was a bundle of white feathers. Tree swallows line their nests with white feathers, and the more feathers they find, the more they use.

"Take the feathers out when there is a breeze," Becky instructed in an enclosed note. "Holding them one by one high in the air, release them into the wind for the birds to snatch."

The package arrived while we were preparing our rooms for the first B&B guests at the sanctuary. I suspended my role as interior decorator and took the feathers to a spot in the garden near the nest boxes. Bed-and-breakfast preparations could wait; I was going out to play with my birds. Plucking a feather from the bag as instructed, I held it over my head and was immediately surrounded by a flood of swirling swallows. I released the feather. As it floated gently away, one of the birds flew in and snatched it up. It peeled away with the treasure— nearly twice its size—streaming behind. Then the bird carried

its white cargo high in the air, let it go, dived to grab it, carried it back up, dropped it, and collected it again. Obviously playing with the feather, the swallow repeated this antic, but the third time it released the feather, another swallow swooped in from below and grabbed it. The interloper took the feather to its nest box, shoved it halfway into the opening, and went inside, dragging the feather in as well.

I held a second feather up; more swallows gathered

overhead and glided in circles waiting for its release. Instead of letting it go, I held it over my head. One swallow descended and hovered like a hummingbird, inches away. Then, with a barely audible snap of its tiny bill, the bird grabbed the white feather and was off to its nest box on the far side of the strawberry patch.

It was an exhilarating experience to interact with these luminous, gregarious little birds. Although I'd intended to release only a few feathers, I ended up emptying the entire bag. Game over, I returned to work and the swallows went back to foraging over our field. Incredibly, the next time I went outdoors I was swamped by swallows looking to me for more feathers. After only a single encounter, they clearly identified me with feathers.

Jimmy picked up another bag in a craft store when he went to town later in the week. We emptied that bag as quickly as the first. The thrill of letting tree swallows pluck feathers from our hands was irresistible. Rationing was out of the question. On his next trip to town, Jimmy cleaned out the store— buying the four bags of white feathers left on the shelves. We then had enough to keep us supplied for the summer, and we continued offering them for as long as the birds would take them.

Once the birds began to feed their young, however, they wanted no part of us. If we got too close to a swallow nest box after the eggs inside hatched, one of the parents would dive-bomb us from behind, turning abruptly away from our heads at the last minute with a small but startling screech. My first swallow attack was so sudden and alarming, it nearly sent me into orbit.

Although, like most other people, we originally put these nest boxes up for eastern bluebirds, swallows have always used most of them because they are colonial nesters. Bluebirds, unlike swallows, are highly territorial and one pair will not nest in close proximity to another. But they will tolerate other species within their territories, so by placing several nest boxes in each section of our fields, we can provide homes for both birds.

Bluebirds are around from early spring until October.

Swallows are here for a much shorter stay. They arrive in April and settle down to nest in May. Their young begin to fledge in the middle of June and, on our property, by the Fourth of July they are virtually all gone. Often the dozen or so pairs we host annually will have completed their nesting cycles before the summer solstice has arrived. When they leave, heralding the end of a summer that hasn't even officially begun, an unwelcome quiet descends over our meadows, even though they are still full of nesting bluebirds and bobolinks, eastern meadowlarks, and several species of sparrows.

Many swallows, however, remain in the area, especially along the shorelines not far from our home. They stay until their migration, which begins in August. It's a behavior we don't yet understand since there is certainly as much food for them here—especially over the wetland—as there is along the lakes.

4

BLUEBIRDS IN A CANNON

The year 1927 was a good one for baseball, aviation, and, as it turned out, our troubled bluebird population. Baseball fans will recognize that year as the one in which Babe Ruth hit sixty home runs, and aviation buffs know that it was also the year Charles Lindbergh crossed the Atlantic in The Spirit of St. Louis.

What few people know is that by 1927 eastern bluebird populations had begun their precipitous decline. The problem was habitat loss and nest-site competition with two avian species introduced from Europe: starlings and house sparrows. But that same year a devoted and most helpful bluebird advocate was born. His name is Frank Zuern.

When he was ten years old, Frank discovered a nesting pair of eastern bluebirds in a hollow fence post on the family farm in Penbine, Wisconsin. The beautiful blue thrushes with the rusty breasts captivated him. At age fourteen, he built his first bluebird nest box. Unfortunately, the nestlings died. Young

Frank was heartbroken. He was also confused, as there was no apparent reason for the chicks' deaths.

The year we moved to northern Michigan, we became friends with Jan and Don Kerr, who operated a bed-and-breakfast in an old home overlooking Lake Leelanau. Don built three nest boxes and mounted them on posts near their garden. Tree swallows took one box, a pair of chickadees used another, and a pair of eastern bluebirds commandeered the third. Jan was able to watch the nesting birds from a window next to her desk. The swallow and chickadee youngsters fledged during the time that the bluebird pair was still feeding their young inside the nest box. One afternoon as Jan watched through her window, the bluebird parents became distressed. They continually flew around the house, poked their heads in, and fussed at the young inside. Not wanting to disturb the family, she did not intervene. By the time Don returned from work, all activity around the box had ceased and the parents were no place to be seen.

Don opened the box and inside found four perfectly formed, fully feathered bluebird nestlings. They were all dead. Jan was devastated. She called me and asked through her tears, "What could have happened to these little birds?"

I did not know any more than Frank Zuern had known forty-six years earlier. Thankfully young Frank had not been deterred by the failure of his first nest box. He persevered, building his nest boxes and monitoring them until eventually he learned that his earlier models had lacked sufficient ventilation. His nestlings—and the Kerr's in later years—had literally cooked inside their homes.

Frank later moved away from the family farm, attended college, and got married. He became a schoolteacher and then a principal. For a time his interest in bluebirds waned. But in the 1970s he renewed his pursuit and once again erected bluebird boxes around the family farm. For ten years his efforts were met largely with success, although he still occasionally lost nestlings to heat. Then, in the 1980s, the raccoon population in Wisconsin exploded, and Frank began to lose increasing numbers of nestlings to predation.

In the summer of 1980, while he and his wife Jane

vacationed in Chickamauga, Georgia, he watched a pair of bluebirds that had built their nest in a Civil War cannon. He was amazed to find bluebirds nesting in such a strange place, and when he returned to Wisconsin he talked to several old-timers about the cannon-nesting bluebirds. They all told him that when they were youngsters they had seen the birds nesting in the hollowed-out ends of broken tree branches. Frank set out to design a box replicating a broken tree branch.

The result was a revolutionary new design, which he called the Tree Branch Bluebird House. It is a bit strange looking to those of us accustomed to the traditional vertical boxes, also called Peterson boxes. Zuern's box is eighteen inches long and has a baffle toward the back, behind which the hen typically places her nest. This design puts the eggs and, when they hatch, the chicks beyond the reach of predators like raccoons and cats. With fifteen large ventilation holes drilled along each side under a wide, overhanging roof, the inside of this box allows plenty of air movement even on the hottest days.

Frank has used his design with great success. In one year alone, he monitored fifty Tree Branch Bluebird Houses he built. Thirty of those houses hosted bluebird pairs, and bluebird chicks fledged successfully from every one.

The year after the Kerrs lost their first bluebird nestlings to heat stroke, Don again put up the vertical boxes he had built. Tragically, the birds suffered the same result. It was not long after that loss that I interviewed Frank for a newspaper column and learned about his revolutionary design. Today the Kerrs successfully use the retired school principal's design, and we, too, have used these boxes on our property. Tree swallows and eastern bluebirds both use them. To date, like the Kerrs and the man who developed this remarkable design, we have never lost a single chick to predators or heat stress.

Editor's Note: For plans on how to build the Tree Branch Blue-bird Box, you can visit the Crofton Creek Press Web page at www.croftoncreek.com.

5

A RARE BIRD

Fred Case—Michigan's acclaimed orchid expert—was our first guest at Charter Sanctuary. He came inside and surveyed our home with interest. Then he followed me into the kitchen, where he ran his hand over the spindled towel bar on the side of an old walnut bachelor's chest.

"I love your antiques," he said approvingly, winning my heart at once.

Fred was widowed the year before and asked if we would object to him using the television in the living room. Since his wife died, he said, he had trouble getting to sleep. Television often bored him enough that he nodded off. I showed him the intricacies of our satellite system, got him a glass of ice for his nightcap—a can of 7-Up—and left the house to him.

The next morning Jimmy left early to help his cousin manage an estate sale for our old neighbor Florence Hanes, who had died suddenly during the winter. I stayed behind—and made an immediate exception for the man who had admired our old furniture. Jimmy and I had agreed that this time around as bed-and-breakfast hosts we would only offer a continental breakfast: juice, croissants, coffee, and homemade jam. Neither of us had time to put together the gourmet meals that had once kept me in the kitchen for as many as seven hours every day. But when Fred arose that morning, I asked what he wanted for breakfast. Although I would have happily put together one of my old recipes for this friendly little man, his request was easy—a single fried egg, warmed croissant with butter and jam, and black coffee.

"I'm not supposed to have this," he said with a satisfied chuckle as he attacked the sunny-side-up egg. Then he polished it off in short order.

While he ate, he talked about his late wife, who had died a year earlier. He spoke of their lives together, the wonderful places they had visited, and the research they had shared.

"My life will never be the same," he said softly when I refilled his coffee mug. "Cherish the time you have together. You never know when it will end."

After he finished his meal, he walked with me into our woods to look for orchids. Just as we crossed the footbridge over the creek, something tumbled across the path ahead of us and vanished into the understory. Something else—or rather some *things* that were much smaller than the first whatever-it-was—skittered off in the other direction. I had no idea what they were, but Fred, who spent so much of his time in woods, recognized them immediately.

"Those were grouse," he said. "Did you see the way the hen rolled off in one direction and the chicks ran off the other way? That roll and tumble was her distraction display."

The previous summer our son Jeff lived next to the house in our motor home. Jeff, a devoted and knowledgeable birder, makes his living leading tours to wild places around the world in search of rare and unusual birds. While he lived next to us, Jeff and I took daily walks in late afternoon or early evening, and we occasionally heard a male ruffed grouse drumming during our outings. Once we even watched him as he stood on

his log, his neck feathers puffed out and his crest raised as he beat his wings rapidly back and forth, producing the drumming sound associated with his territorial displays. But neither Jeff nor I had ever seen a hen. Now here she was with her brood.

Not wanting to distress the family further, Fred and I turned around immediately. On the way back, the orchid man found what he was looking for alongside the path. It was of European origin. We had talked earlier about exotics—plants, animals, and birds introduced from other countries that often wreak havoc on our own flora and fauna—and had agreed that wherever possible, they should be eliminated. But Fred loved orchids and would make an exception for the single plant he found in our woods.

"Don't take it out," he said. "It's very beautiful."

I saw him off reluctantly, got ready for work, and stopped at Florence's home on my way through town. The night before had seen the kick-off for the village's sesquicentennial celebration. Birthday cake and ice cream followed a re-enactment of the arrival of the first Europeans performed by descendants of local Native Americans and white settlers. The town was full of flowers and flags and high spirits when I wedged my car in among the dozens in front of Florence's home and walked through the open door. My own mood, however, was not so cheerful; it was the first time I'd been in her home since she died.

Florence and I had become friends when Jimmy and I owned the old Victorian house that was our first foray into the bed-and-breakfast business. Florence lived across the side street. The Victorian had been built by the town's first doctor, who came north following his discharge from the army after the Civil War. Dr. Stephen Hutchinson, a bit of a Renaissance man, was interested in botany as well as biology and had filled his property—which was just over seven acres at the time—with trees and shrubs from around the world.

We called our place "Hutchinson's Garden," in honor of its first owner. It was there that I saw for the first time a brown-headed cowbird chick being fed by a host species—in this case a song sparrow. It was also there that we got our first look at an ovenbird—after it crashed into our window and killed itself. We took lessons from each experience. Cowbirds are unwelcome on our property. As for window kills, we used windows with outside screens in our next two homes; screens reduce the reflected image of outdoor habitat, thereby reducing crashes. The screens also cushion the blow for those birds that do fly into the windows. So far, not one of the few birds that have crashed into the screens has even been visibly stunned.

When we bought the old house, only about an acre and a half of the original property remained. Around the grounds were the remnants of Dr. Hutchinson's famous plantings, among them an enormous copper beech whose branches spread over most of the side yard. Our dining room window looked out on that beech tree. So did the window over Florence's tiny kitchen table, where she spent much of her time.

Florence already knew Jimmy when we bought the place. Though she was a fair number of years older, they had both grown up in the village and her father had worked as a carpenter with Jimmy's grandfather. The population was small and everyone knew everyone else. She was pleased when we bought the house and began to spruce it up. Florence was raised by her widowed father in an old two-story house a stone's throw from the newer single-story home she lived in when we became her neighbors. As a child she had spent a great deal of time in the yard around the Hutchinson house with the groundskeeper who had befriended her. She was delighted that Jimmy was undertaking at least a partial restoration of the grounds.

I met her during our first summer when she brought over a bowl of her precious boysenberries to share with us. I didn't learn until later that it was a special gesture; Florence didn't share much. She didn't have much to share. When I took her a plate of cookies in return, she invited me in. That was an even more significant gesture—she never invited people into her home.

Florence was a bit of an odd duck, a true eccentric. She was a literal string saver. On one of my visits to her home, she came to the door drying her hair with a threadbare towel. A bit embarrassed that I'd caught her with her head wrapped in a piece of cloth most of us would think had gone beyond the rag stage, she said, "I don't know why I keep using these old towels when I have brand new ones in the drawer."

I told her she ought to use her nice new ones; she deserved it.

"I really should," she agreed.

But she never did. Florence was also a pack rat. At the time of her death, her home was so filled with stuff it was nearly impossible to move through it. Costume jewelry hung from tie racks on two walls in her bedroom, and she had shoeboxes filled with earrings, pins, and necklaces. She had forty winter coats—though she seldom left her home—three full sets of dishes, and forty-one skillets. This for one small, solitary soul who lived on cookies and canned soup, supplemented by the summertime product of her little garden.

Florence had a wonderful self-deprecating sense of humor and a hearty laugh. She was extremely private, but very outspoken when engaged. Though our personalities were polar opposites—she was a near recluse and I am almost compulsively social—our minds ran along parallel tracks and we enjoyed our conversations together. I considered it a great compliment that I was always welcome in her home and was often taken into her confidence.

She became something of a bird watcher herself as our friendship grew, and she nearly always had a question about this or that unfamiliar bird that showed up in her yard. She clipped every article she could find on birds and saved the clippings for me. Florence especially liked crows. She recognized their intelligence and appreciated their company. Every day she held something out from her meager rations for the four big black birds that landed in her front yard after supper to gather up her offerings. She knew I wasn't as fond of crows as she was; their habit of raiding our songbird nests troubled me.

"Now don't you say anything bad about my crows," she warned. "They are my friends."

I would never have said anything bad about Florence's feathered friends.

She had, among her old treasures, a book of Audubon prints. One day when I went to visit, she presented it to me as a special gift. She was afraid that when she died it would go on the trash heap, and she wanted it to go to someone who would appreciate it.

Florence also clipped recipes, and she loved to talk about food preparation, in spite of the fact that she had never been— by her own admission—a cook. One afternoon when I was sitting at the chair beside her table—which was piled high with newspapers, magazines, and clippings of all kinds—a cottontail hopped into the open in her yard.

"Yum-m-m," she said when she spotted the bunny. "Hasenpfeffer. Doesn't that sound good for dinner?"

When Florence hankered for hasenpfeffer at the sight of the bunny, she knew what she was talking about. Over the course of her life, she had prepared many rabbits for her table, even if she wasn't especially interested in cooking. In her day, Florence handled a mean shotgun. Her father scraped for a living during her young years and, like many people who live close to nature, he had supplemented garden-grown food with what little he could buy and, no doubt, what he could shoot. When she grew up, she became a good hunter in her own right. Her late husband had been a hunter, and she loved to tell and retell tales of their camping and hunting adventures.

Florence refused to judge anyone else's behavior, and when others around her did, she took them to task for it. Not long after we met, controversy arose in the local press over a public official's private life in nearby Traverse City. Florence's position was clear and absolute: "This man's life is nobody's business but his."

After the barn fire sent all our possessions up in smoke, she gave me several cookbooks. One of them was a copy of *The Joy of Cooking*, which had been given to her by Ruth Bobbs, wife of the book's publisher. Florence had worked for the Bobbs family during their summer stays at their cottage on Northport Point.

In the middle of that last winter, she learned that she had a form of fast-growing breast cancer. The week after she heard this awful news, Jimmy's cousin, Jean Putnam, was to take her for a test. When Jean arrived at the house, however, there was no response to her knock. After checking with the local hospital to see if Florence had gone ahead, Jean finally broke into the house. She found my friend sitting in her bed, where she had died during the night.

More than anything else, Florence didn't want to be a bother or a burden to anyone. It is entirely possible that she simply decided it was time to go with grace and then left the body that had betrayed her with a terrible illness. She didn't take anything to hasten the process, but she was a fan of Dr. Kevorkian and she was determined enough that if she made up her mind it was time to go, she would have done exactly that.

When I stopped at her estate sale, her cramped little house was full of locals, many of whom were far more interested in prowling around inside than they were in finding a bargain.

"Look at all these dishes," one woman said.

And from another, "Can you believe she had all this stuff?"

"I've always wanted to see what was inside of this house..."

I couldn't stay. It was too hard to watch strangers picking over the remnants of my old friend's life. I felt as though these townsfolk—most of whom I know and like—had suddenly become vultures.

I hadn't intended to buy anything, but on the way out an old five-gallon crock with the image of Illinois on the side of it caught my eye. Florence had lived for a few years in Illinois, which is my home state. It seemed a fitting remembrance to have in our home. I asked Jimmy to get it for me. It now sits next to my desk as a permanent reminder of my departed friend.

6

OF REDSTARTS
AND GROSBEAKS

Our next-door neighbor when we lived on the bay was a bachelor named Dave Brigham. Dave was a kind man with a creative streak who managed to survive for years without punching the proverbial clock—at least not on a regular basis. He built his unique but modest three-story cedar home with his own hands—bit by bit as he was financially able. Then he filled it with an eclectic mix of antiques and odds and ends. Dave's home featured a window wall stretching nearly the width of the main floor that provided him with an incredible view of the water.

Dave was a nature lover, and although he was not what you'd call a birder, he knew many of the birds that frequented the forest around him. He occasionally joined us for toast and coffee before starting his day. One morning as he sat across from me cradling his steaming mug, he asked about a bird he couldn't identify. He said he had heard it every summer since he bought his property.

"I've never been able to find this bird," he said. "But I hear it all the time. It must be kind of big because it has such a loud voice...it sounds like it's singing down a rain barrel."

I told him I'd never heard a more perfect description of a singing veery. Plain little thrushes, veeries are summertime denizens of dense understory. From the time we moved into the house next to Dave's, at least one pair regularly nested in the woods behind our two homes. It was there he had heard the male's song, a downward spiral of flutelike notes, during the nesting season.

Even though Dave couldn't identify every songbird on his property, he watched them carefully and was aware of the decline of some species. Also aware that habitat loss was largely to blame, he was disturbed by the growing development that destroyed the forests around him. He especially mourned the loss of the scarlet tanagers that once nested in his yard's old trees every year.

Dave was also distressed by the fact that his wonderful window wall was a bird killer. He estimated that as many as two dozen songbirds were killed annually by crashing into the glass. It had reached the point that he felt guilty about installing the window in the first place.

"I can't stand this," he said to us after a red-eyed vireo crashed and died. "If I'd had any idea this would be the result when I designed my home, I would have done it differently."

The year after we moved in, we created a free-form garden full of flowers and shrubs for hummingbirds and butterflies. On a quiet spring morning I sat alongside the path pulling weeds from one of the beds and a female American redstart landed at the end of the bed. The small, gray warbler with splashes of yellow on her sides, wings, and tail was a pale imitation of her brilliant orange-and-black mate, but she was beautiful nevertheless.

She busied herself with a thin blade of grass that stuck out of the weed pile I had left behind. Taking the blade in her tiny bill, she tried to fly off with it, but she was unable to extricate it. The other end was tightly tangled in the mass. After several failed attempts to snag her prize, she left that

blade for another, which she carried up to her nearly finished nest on a nearby cedar branch. Landing inside the nest, she carefully stitched the grass into the interior. Then, using the force of her body, she pressed her plump belly down and slowly rotated to shape the walls and bottom.

The finished product was a natural work of art. The outside of the compact cup was fashioned from course grasses and ornamented with bits of lichen. The inside was lined with fine grasses and a single small white feather. It was an amazingly sturdy little affair, secured to the top of the branch with delicate plant fibers.

After she finished her work, she laid four eggs inside and then spent most of the next couple of weeks incubating them. When the chicks hatched, her mate joined in the search for the teeny insects needed by their hatchlings. The day after the redstart pair began feeding their young, I was again working in the garden. A red squirrel started up the trunk of the tree that held the nest, and the parents fussed frantically at the intruder in an effort to run it off. When I saw what they were fussing over, I picked up a rake and ran to the tree to scare off the squirrel. It was a temporary victory; the next day the nest was empty. Sometime during my absence from the yard, the four babies had been nabbed—probably by the same squirrel I had terrorized the day before.

The little hen immediately built another nest in a different tree some distance from the first. This time a squirrel got to her eggs before they even hatched. She never tried again. Like most Neotropical songbirds (birds that winter in the tropics and come north to nest and raise their young), her window of opportunity was limited. With the loss of her second nest, it closed. In September our lovely pair of redstarts left for Costa Rica without the offspring needed to ensure the future of their species.

Like our friend Florence Hanes, some of the food Dave brought to his table was collected with his rifle. For the most part he hunted small game like rabbits and grouse. Also, like all good hunters, Dave only shot what he was going to eat. But the year after our redstart nest failed, Dave decided he had had it with the red squirrels, and he aimed his .22 at every one that crossed his path, even though he didn't intend to use them for food. By his own count, he eliminated at least thirty of the furry rodents from our immediate neighborhood that summer. He did so to the benefit of our nesting songbirds. Not only did the American redstarts nest successfully that year, but other species did, too.

When Fred Case and I walked through the woods on our sanctuary, he commented on the absence of squirrels. I told him about the nesting redstarts in the yard of our previous home and Dave's gun. It was a lesson we took to our new property. Numerous pairs of redstarts now nest on our sanctuary every year, and they need not fear that squirrels will raid their nests. As soon as we moved to the sanctuary, I bought a pellet gun. Since then I have eliminated every squirrel that has found its way onto the property.

Eventually I wore my gun out. It was just an inexpensive plastic-stocked model purchased from a local discount store; longevity wasn't in its genes. To replace it, Jimmy bought me a fine German-made model—a Diana—with a heavy wooden stock. It was a beautiful gun that cost about five times what my little Crossman had. It was definitely manufactured to go the distance.

Three days after the Diana arrived, I got a call from a friend who had a bird that had crashed into her window. I asked her what kind it was; she didn't know. It was black and white, she said. Its breast was streaked and it had some yellowish feathers on its neck. It was still alive but seriously injured. She worked at night, and the bird had hit the window as she was getting ready to turn in for the day. I told her to put the bird in a shoebox on her porch and Jimmy and I would pick it up.

When we collected the box, we found a fledgling rose-breasted grosbeak inside. The young bird could raise its head and flutter one wing slightly, but it could not get up and definitely could not fly. A spot of blood stained the box underneath its head. It was clear that the bird's back was broken.

"It will have to be euthanized," I told Jimmy sadly. "There are no wonderful Dr. Robertos for grosbeaks like there was for you."

But my tenderhearted mate begged for a stay.

"Let's give it a chance," he pleaded. "Maybe it'll get better if we keep it quiet overnight."

So we put the beautiful, broken bird in the crawl space under the house—out of the way of predators—for the night. The next morning I went down to check on it. When I brought the box out into the light, the grosbeak raised its head weakly and fluttered a wing slightly, but it could not get up.

Unwilling to allow the bird to suffer a slow, lingering demise, I got my gun, put the barrel against its head, and pulled the trigger. Then I made my way back into the house, buried my head in Jimmy's shoulder, and wept. It broke my heart to have to destroy a fatally injured songbird. But the real tragedy is that every year tens of millions of birds die from window crashes in this country alone.

7

LAZARUS

The weekend after Florence's sale, our B&B home was fully booked, meaning our two rooms had been rented for both nights. Our guests were scheduled to arrive Friday afternoon.

The morning began badly when I turned on my computer to finish a column that was due. A few minutes later, the machine locked up when I tried to save my work. I could neither reboot it nor shut it down. When a hard reboot failed, I pulled out the battery hoping the induced coma would break the spell. That worked, but when I fired it up again, it had completely digested the story I was writing.

It wasn't the first time I'd had trouble with this magic machine. Working with it has been, from the beginning, very much a mixed blessing. While it unquestionably eases writing—or, rather, it eases the process of rewriting—in general it is a vastly more complicated machine than I need. Since, like most people, I understand none of the software and know only enough of the barest basics to use it as a glorified typewriter, I am always on the edge of losing control and continually infuriated when it does take off on its own tangent. On more than one occasion I've threatened to throw it in the lake. But the morning of our first big weekend, I didn't want to drown the damn thing. I e-mailed a hunter friend for help:

> Dear Marn,
>
> My computer needs a major adjustment. Please bring your shotgun.
>
> Thanks,
> Kay

Then I went to wash a load of clothes before our guests arrived with their inevitable need for hot water from our limited supply. When the washer emptied after the wash cycle, the water gurgled up into the bathtub. The septic pump had died. Like most septic systems, water from our home drains by way of gravity into a large concrete tank. Because none of the land near the house "percs" (which means that it doesn't percolate because layers of clay prevent the water from seeping through), the drain field is above our garden—about a hundred linear feet from the house and ten feet higher than the septic tank. Our septic tank overflows into a holding tank instead of directly into a drainfield. Once the holding tank is full, a pump automatically comes on and forces the effluent up into the drain field. The effect of a failed pump can hardly be overstated; no septic system means no flushing, no dishwashing, no showers. In a word, no paying guests.

We had five hours to fix it.

I called the pumper service and Jimmy immediately began digging since both tanks would have to be opened to empty their contents. The woman who answered the phone at the pumper service was understanding and sympathetic. She would, she said, send the pumper out as soon as the driver returned from the job he was on.

It began to mist. Half an hour later, while my mate still shoveled, the mist morphed into rain, and the woman from the pump service called back to say that her driver would be delayed. He wouldn't come, she said, until after it stopped raining. I hung up the phone, headed for the barn to close the doors against the rain, and prayed for a miracle. On the way I found one. Actually there were two.

A month earlier Jimmy had dug up a maple sapling from a thicket south of the house, where it was choked by dense wetland growth. But because the roots were knotted and tangled with other roots, he was unable to get at them. Determined to have his tree, he simply chopped them off and planted the stump next to the driveway near the barn.

"That poor tree will never survive," I said.

"Why not?"

"Because you cut its feet off and put it in a totally different environment than the one it is used to."

"It'll be okay," he said.

The tree promptly lost its leaves and died. I asked him to pull it up and throw it on the brush pile.

"Why should I do that?" he asked.

"Because it's dead."

"That tree is fine."

It wasn't fine; it was dead. And for a month it stayed dead. But as I hurried past this dead tree on my way to close the garage doors, I saw that it was covered with what looked like buds. Closer inspection revealed that the buds were tiny maple leaves. I was amazed that this thing had come back to life, and in honor of its miraculous resurrection, I named it "Lazarus."

At the barn there was another surprise. When we returned from our winter travels at the end of April that year, our eastern phoebes had already set up housekeeping. Their bowl-shaped nest—fashioned from grasses, mud, and moss—rested on a ledge under the eave of the barn. In early May I checked the nest for cowbird eggs and found none. Instead four perfect little white phoebe eggs lay cradled in the bottom.

The eastern phoebes are special to us. We are like parents who have waited longer than expected for much-anticipated babies. It took three years for a pair of these handsome little flycatchers to discover the ledge Jimmy built and mounted for them under the eave of our barn. Once they found it, however, they used it to good advantage, producing two clutches of plump offspring every summer—adding a total of fourteen individuals to the overall population of eastern phoebes in their first two years here.

The day after I checked the nest, Jimmy noted that the female wasn't foraging around the barn as was her habit. He also saw that her mate spent the afternoon alternately calling for her and checking their nest in the hope of finding her. For several days the male continued to call and search for the hen. Finally he gave up and left.

Because our home and barn sit in the center of our forty-seven acres, it was unlikely that the little female had become a victim of an encounter with a vehicle. And because the nest was under a wide eave, it was equally unlikely that she had fallen prey to a nocturnal mammalian predator. The greatest likelihood was that a sharp-shinned or Cooper's hawk took her while she was foraging for insects.

I kept the nest, even though it is against the law to possess the nest of any bird. It is a good law and I believe in its purpose, which is to protect nesting birds against unscrupulous collectors. But when we lose something we care deeply about, it helps to have a physical reminder. So I violated the law I firmly support, put the nest in a plastic bag, and tucked it away. And, with a heavy heart, I accepted the reality that this year no phoebes would fledge from our property.

Two weeks after the male left, another pair of phoebes arrived and took over the ledge. Days passed and there was no nesting material, in spite of the fact that the pair made many trips up to the ledge. Then the hen began to sit on it for long periods. Because there was no nest, Jimmy and I decided the pair was too young to know how to go about raising a family and was just going through the motions in an avian version of playing house. But after I passed the born-again maple tree on the day our septic pump failed, I glanced up at the ledge as I reached for the garage door and was startled to see three baby phoebe faces peering back down at me. If I was pleasantly surprised by the revived maple, I was ecstatic about these three little birds. I took the happy news back to Jimmy, who was still shoveling dirt.

The pumper truck finally arrived to empty the tanks, and Jimmy picked up a new pump from our local excavation company. Half an hour before our guests arrived, the new pump was installed and tested, and the holes in the earth filled in.

Because our home has only two bedrooms, Jimmy and I had to sleep in our old motor home when we had guests. That night, when we went out to the motor home to turn in, I saw that one of the phoebe nestlings had fallen from the ledge onto the barn's concrete apron. I picked him up and put him back where he belonged while Jimmy found a piece of scrap carpet to put under the ledge in case there were any further mishaps. It's a good thing he did. When we got up the next morning, the chick was back down. Once again I put him back on the ledge. When we found him back on the carpet scrap the third time, we decided he must have been falling off the ledge because there was no nest to prevent him from tumbling out. I retrieved the original nest from its plastic bag, put the chick in it, and climbed a ladder to collect the other two nestlings.

From eye level, I could see that the hen had laid her eggs not on the bare wooden ledge but on a grass and moss rug she had created for her nestlings. I scooped up the two babies in one hand and pulled the mossy mat from the ledge with the other. As I did so, a swarm of tiny red mites emerged from the mat and covered my arm. Our little bird hadn't fallen out of his nest; he had jumped to escape a mite infestation.

Jimmy quickly removed an unused ledge from the back side of the house and mounted it on the barn a few feet away. Then he placed the nestlings' new home on it. After the babies were safely tucked into their new surroundings, I poured boiling water over the moss-mat to kill the parasites and then went back into the house to wait for the parents to find their kids.

It took the adults about ten minutes to figure out that their family had been moved. When they did, they continued to feed them as though nothing had happened. One or the other kept an eye on the nest from the tree named Lazarus between foraging and feeding duties.

Less than a week after we moved the nest, three healthy phoebe fledglings left their nest for good, becoming numbers fifteen, sixteen, and seventeen from Charter Sanctuary.

8

CHICK-SITTING AN
ENDANGERED SPECIES

Sitting on a file cabinet behind my desk is a photo of four human hands holding an equal number of downy gray-and-white
chicks with tiny sharp bills and round black eyes. On the back
of the photo are printed the words, "Thank you for caring!" It
is signed "The Cathead Bay Piping Plovers," and below the
signature is the penciled drawing of two tiny bird feet. The
photo was a gift from a young man named Nick Torsky, a State
of Michigan biologist who worked on behalf of the birds for
three summers.

Great Lakes piping plovers are highly endangered little
shorebirds struggling to maintain a hold on survival. There are
three distinct populations of piping plovers: one nests in the
Great Plains, another along the Atlantic Coast, and the third
around the Great Lakes. All three populations are seriously
troubled, but the Great Lakes birds are the most severely endangered. It is estimated that this population once numbered

as high as six hundred to eight hundred pairs. Early in the last century, the birds were threatened by market hunting. With protection, they began to bounce back by the middle of the century. Then, for some reason, the numbers began to slump again. In 1979 only thirty-eight pairs remained. When the Great Lakes birds were listed as endangered in 1986, there were only seventeen known nesting pairs, and by 1990 a mere twelve pairs were recorded.

One of the reasons for their critically reduced numbers is, as with many other creatures, loss of habitat. Piping plovers prefer open sandy beaches with sparse vegetation and scattered cobble for nesting. During the last half of the twentieth century that kind of habitat was increasingly coveted by our own species for recreation and development. The beach at Cathead Bay is perfect habitat for these little birds, and it is protected from development because it is part of Leelanau State Park. It is also relatively remote and can only be reached by hiking nearly a mile through the woods. For the most part, the birds can nest there with little human interference.

Habitat loss is not the piping plovers' only problem. They are even struggling in places where suitable nest habitat is largely isolated from all development, as it is on Cathead Bay. The other problem for the plovers is a dramatic rise in several predator species that either target them or come upon them unexpectedly. Species that prey on piping plovers include coyotes, raccoons, ring-billed gulls, crows, ground squirrels, and household pets. The rise in the populations of all of these creatures may explain why these birds continued to lose ground after they were listed as endangered.

Nesting piping plovers disappeared from Cathead Bay for nearly a decade. Then two pairs settled down on the beach in 1997. Jimmy and I immediately volunteered to be "chick-sitters." It was our job to help educate the public about the plovers, to inform visitors with dogs that their pets weren't allowed on the beach, and to dissuade gulls or crows that landed too near the foraging families. Plover chicks are unable to fly until they are three to four weeks old. Because they forage frequently at the water's edge, where there is no cover, they are

exceedingly vulnerable until they can fly.

Our first day on the job came during the Fourth of July weekend. With a daypack filled with reading material, lunch, and drinking water, we hiked out the long wooded trail that ends high on a wide, sparsely vegetated drumlin dune overlooking horseshoe-shaped Cathead Bay. It is one of the most spectacularly beautiful dunes in the country. From there we trudged northwest through the fine sand and then turned due north along the beach.

Half a mile from the woods, we reached the place where we had been told the seven chicks would be foraging with their parents in the wet sand along the water's edge. Although we searched for the birds for several hours, we found neither chicks nor adults. Several days later we learned that we were too late; something had already taken the chicks. Once the chicks were gone, the adults dispersed.

The following year, three pairs of plovers nested on Cathead. Nick, who had worked at another plover site the year before, volunteered to serve as onsite head of the recovery effort. The first thing he did was to locate and "exclose" each of the nests. Exclosures are fencing placed around the nest site to keep predators out but allow the adults free access. These devices have been used successfully for a number of years to prevent egg loss and have increased hatching success from as low as 30 percent to nearly 95 percent. Once the eggs hatch, the chicks leave the exclosure to forage under the watchful eyes of their parents. They do not return.

Once Nick had the exclosures in place, he cordoned off a broad area of the dunes encompassing all three nests and posted it with "Endangered Species" notices.

Just after the first nest hatched, I went out on the beach to interview the young biologist for an article about the birds. I had little spare time that year and hadn't intended to work as a chick-sitter again, but Nick's personal dedication and commitment to the birds was persuasive. Before I left, I signed on for another stint.

All four birds from the first nest hatched and they were still scurrying around the beach when the four eggs from the second nest hatched two weeks later. At that point, hopes were very high for a successful summer for the Cathead plovers. Unfortunately, only three of those eight chicks were still alive when chicks in the third and final nest hatched. Still, all of us who worked with the birds consoled ourselves with the thought that if four chicks survived from the third nest, we would see seven new plovers added to the Great Lakes population—a respectable increase.

Two days after the final four chicks hatched, three members of the piping plover recovery team from the University of Michigan Biological Station came to help Nick band the chicks. I wanted to watch the banding process, but because there were no other volunteers, I stayed on the beach while the team went inside the closed area. While doing guard duty, I chased a few gulls, talked to a couple hiking across the beach, and asked three young men in a boat if they would move away from the closed area.

It was a long time before the team members came back from the dunes. When they did, Nick came up to me and said that something had taken five of the birds. The hen and all four of her chicks were gone. Gone as in eaten. Gone as in gobbled down. A predator had simply taken these five rare treasures for a light snack between nine o'clock the previous evening and nine that morning.

The three team members from the Biological Station left, and Nick and I sat on the beach for a long time without speaking. As the two of us sat in silence, I couldn't erase the image of the beautiful little mother trying desperately to defend her chicks from being eaten alive and, in the process, becoming a victim herself.

The loss was no less devastating for the young man sitting next to me who had worked so hard to prevent exactly that result. During the previous six weeks, Nick had taken only one full day off, often making the nearly hour-long drive from Traverse City to check on the birds and their volunteer sitters on his own time.

At first I was hurt. Then I was angry. The loss of the last nest demonstrated the tremendous obstacle to this bird's recovery—excessive predation. It is a factor that those in charge of the program aren't even considering. Even if Great Lakes piping plovers reach two hundred pairs—which researchers believe would be a self-sustaining population—without the constant protection of bird sitters and biologists, predators would inevitably decimate the birds once again. Excessive predation for the plovers has created a nearly insurmountable challenge to their ultimate survival.

The relationship between predator and prey is essential. Predators are not "bad" animals; without them, prey species would become overpopulated. In a balanced ecosystem, however, predators are subject to their own population controls. Currently, raccoons and coyotes are abundant—some would say overabundant—in Leelanau County, as well as in other parts of the country. Both of these species feed on the eggs and chicks of nesting birds, and both prowl Cathead Bay beach in significant numbers every night. Unfortunately, there are currently no other species making meals of coyotes and raccoons.

After large predators like cougars and wolves were extirpated, it was largely hunters and trappers who exerted population controls for midsized predators like the ones wreaking havoc on Leelanau's plovers. But the successful campaign against fur has removed the impact of hunting and trapping on these species. The result has been devastating not just for this beautiful little shorebird but for other creatures as well.

When I talked to a friend about my trauma, she asked if I could kill a raccoon. I asked her if she could kill a cobra in the nursery. She didn't understand the analogy. I explained: In the scheme of things, an individual piping plover is no more or less important than an individual raccoon. By the same token, however, raccoons as a species are no more important than piping plovers. The survival of *all* species is essential if we are to maintain the fascinating biodiversity we are blessed with. But many species will not survive if we continue to ignore the need to manage out-of-control populations of animals that are decimating other species.

Could I take aim at a cuddly looking, furry raccoon? I wish I'd had the chance on behalf of the beautiful little plover hen and her two-day-old chicks.

9

BROKEN PROMISE

The following nesting season brought only two plover pairs to Cathead Bay. Nick was again on duty. He immediately exclosed the nest sites and began his long days of documentation.

The federal official who headed up the U.S. Endangered Species Program in Michigan called in mid-May and asked me to meet with her. I agreed and we set a date. She was coming north with a young biologist-intern so that the two of them could spend a weekend on nearby North Manitou Island to check on plover nests there. The three of us talked about the problems for the birds while we hiked the long trail out to the Cathead nest site, and I expressed frustration over the predation problem there. I said that a mere three fledged chicks out of twelve hatchlings was an unacceptable result.

"There were seven fledglings from this beach," the official said.

"There were three."

She challenged my number again. I struggled to control the pain and anger that bubbled to the surface on behalf of the lost birds from the previous season. When I spoke again, my voice was tight with emotion.

"I was with these birds nearly every day last year," I said. "And I can assure you that only three chicks fledged from this beach."

She tossed her long blonde curls back from her face and said lightly, "Oh well, it could have been none."

I could have hit her.

"Extinction is a very ugly word," I said through my anger. "But if we don't resolve the predator problem for these birds, they aren't going to make it in the long run. And it will be our fault for not protecting them."

The fact that she was unaware of the devastating statistics generated a huge knot in my gut. It was her job to establish the guidelines that would protect these birds, but how could she do what was right by them if she didn't understand what they were up against?

She and her intern left the next morning for North Manitou Island. The island is reached by a ferry that calls only once a day, and during bad weather, it doesn't leave the mainland at all. The two women got caught during a storm and were not able to return when they had planned. The extra time on the island allowed them to gather additional data. Once they were back on the mainland, the Endangered Species Program official stopped by the lighthouse gift shop where I was working to tell me that she was shocked at the abundance of raccoon tracks she and her intern had seen on North Manitou. Before she left, she assured me that something would be done to protect the birds.

My job at the gift shop and our B&B duties made it impossible for me to volunteer that summer, but I did call Dave Barrons, a local television meteorologist who is also a birder, and asked if he would include a bit about the birds in one of his regular outdoor features. All of us who have worked with the plovers believe that part of the problem is a lack of public awareness. We believed that if people knew more about them, like they do about the Kirtland's warbler and the peregrine falcon, they would pressure the government to take the steps necessary to save them. The year before I wrote several pieces for the local daily paper about the plovers plight and persuaded the reporter for our public radio station to do a story about them.

Television seemed the next logical step. Thus the call to Barrons, who said that he would be happy to include a piece about them. We scheduled a shoot on the beach for the following Friday. The day before we were to go out to the nesting area for the television piece, Nick came into the shop.

"No chicks," he said.

All of the babies had been depredated. My relief came into the shop and I went outdoors with Nick.

"Do you want me to call the station for you?" he asked.

I nodded numbly.

Seven eggs had hatched. Seven chicks had been eaten. None would have been more than a few days old. That evening, when I got home, I e-mailed the intern who had gone to the island with the federal official.

> Hi Christie,
>
> I don't know whether or not you heard the news, but the seven chicks that hatched on Cathead over the last

two weeks are gone. It was a crushing blow for all concerned. Think of it, of twenty-six healthy hatchlings on that one beach over the past three years, only three have matured to fledge. This is the last year I'll be involved; I simply cannot bear the pain. Future years will find me focusing on our songbirds here at home, who—you can rest assured—will not fight the predator problem the plovers do. I have determined that I won't even ask about the plovers. Without changes in policy, the future for the birds—at least on that beach—is bleak. I wish there were a way to sign Cathead, in wording the birds would understand, that they should avoid that place because it means almost certain death for the chicks they work so hard to produce. It was really nice to meet you, and I hope we can meet again under happier circumstances.

Best regards,
Kay Charter

She e-mailed back immediately:

Hello Kay,

I am saddened by your news about the plover chicks at Cathead Bay. I know how frustrating and depressing it is to see chicks disappearing from the beach. When I was monitoring and protecting plovers in Grand Marais, Michigan, I saw the same thing happen. In fact one day, while I was watching, a crow flew down from a nearby perch and snatched a plover chick. I stood up and ran after the culprit, but it was too late. Within a week the whole brood was gone. It was very painful, especially when I knew exactly what the problem was and I could not do anything about it. This crow predation happened on the same beach for several years, but finally the birds got smart and moved to a new beach. I definitely understand your frustration! I can appreciate why you would want to distance yourself from such a seemingly fruitless task. However, I remind you that when it comes to piping plover protection and success it is caring local individuals, people like yourself, that make a huge difference. Your caring and dedication has been instrumental in making people aware of the problems facing plovers at Cathead Bay. Maybe your input along with the unsuccessful nests again this year will help change policies at Cathead Bay. Hang in there, I think you will see some changes in the near future. Take care and thanks for the update!

Sincerely,
C. D.

A few weeks later I talked to the federal official again. The intern had forwarded my message to her. The official said she felt like I was throwing rocks at her. She was right to feel that way.

She has since moved on, and the last I heard the position had not been filled. For the sake of the piping plovers, when it is, I hope it is with someone who has a passion for the birds he or she is charged with saving. If it becomes clear that the state and federal governments are serious about providing the plovers with a genuine chance, I will again join the ranks of chick-sitters. But if things don't change, no amount of schmoozing from people like C.D. will draw me back out to Cathead Bay beach to watch over downy plover chicks that will inevitably be eaten by predators that are out of control.

10

BIRD WITH THE UPSIDE-DOWN BRAIN

Songbirds aren't the only avian order that occurs on our sanctuary. Red-tailed hawks and northern harriers regularly hunt over our fields, and owls haunt our woods. American kestrels, the smallest raptors on the continent, raised families in the nest box we provided for two summers. These helmeted, plump little hawks would still be here if we hadn't moved their box. When we realized they were taking our killdeer chicks to feed their own offspring, we moved the box well away from the upland meadow. But the colorful raptors didn't find the new location to their liking and left the property altogether.

Mallards nest near the marsh and wood ducks feed in our flooded wetland in the spring. Hairy and downy woodpeckers are resident throughout the year, and a pair of northern flickers produced healthy youngsters in spite of the blasted starlings. I looked out the window one morning and there they were, a family of six, hopping through the rough grass in our lawn with their comical, humping gait, probing the dirt for ants. During the time Jeff lived in our motor home, he watched a young bald eagle forage on a deer carcass—a doe that had lost her race with a passing car—at the edge of our drive.

Then there are shorebirds, marsh birds, and waders. On the first Mother's Day after we moved into our home, a common snipe foraged at the muddy edge of the creek through the wetland. A week later a solitary sandpiper was in the same place, and the following month two pairs of Virginia rails took up residence in our cattails—one pair at each end of the long, narrow wetland. In more recent years, a pair of soras has also nested there. Imagine coming around the corner of your home and finding a bird you don't recognize venturing onto the grass beside a wet thicket and finding out that what you have seen in your yard is a sora chick.

Every year has brought nesting killdeer to our upland meadows, a great blue heron roosted up in the pin cherries along the east side of our home while we were building it, and each year a pair of green herons take minnows from the creek.

Then there are American woodcock. The first fledglings we saw after moving to our new property were not songbirds but rather four woodcock chicks—tiny carbon copies of the mother they were following. The mother bird led her fat little all-belly-and-beak youngsters out of our wetland early one May morning, across an open grassy area below the kitchen, and into the damp woods just south of the house. They were a comical fivesome shuffling through the short spring grass before disappearing into the understory.

Every spring since, a woodcock hen has nested near the trail at the back of our wetland. We have never closed the trail because of her nest, but when she is on it we do scuttle tour visitors quickly and quietly past in order to limit impact on the incubating mother.

Woodcock are chunky, short-legged, blunt-winged little birds. Although it is a member of the sandpiper family, this shorebird abandoned the coastal haunts of its relatives eons ago in favor of wet woodlands, moist thickets, and shrubby swamps. Astonishing adaptations occurred along the way.

Today's woodcock has traded the long legs and pointed wings of its ancestors for stubby legs and rounded wings. Most incredible are the changes in the bird's brain. Over time the eyes enlarged and rotated back from the beak. They are now located high on the skull, providing it with a nearly 360-degree range of vision that enables it to watch for predators both front and back while foraging. As the eyes moved, the brain tilted backwards so that the cerebellum is now forward of the cerebral hemispheres. Thus the woodcock is the only bird said to have an "upside-down brain."

A mottled bird of many colors, woodcock are a wonder of camouflage. Stripes and spots of brown, tan, gray, and black cover the bird's back and head. Its belly is a soft rust. A hen incubating her nest in leaf litter at the edge of a woods is virtually impossible to see. This cryptic coloration makes it possible for her to stick to her incubation duties when humans approach.

One summer a woodcock chose our boardwalk through the wetland as its daytime roost. Afternoons it emerged from the shadow of tall, dense cattails whose tops arch over the boardwalk and then padded across a mowed, narrow path to the edge of our newly planted thicket. It always stopped next to a short clump of cedars and began probing the earth, which Jimmy kept freshly turned for its exclusive benefit. There the woodcock searched for earthworms with its very long bill. After each spate of foraging, it would move to another place, scooting around in a half circle, fanning its short tail as it turned. Every afternoon, we watched the bird from inside our kitchen as it scooted around the plowed earth, probing for worms.

The bird's close-set eyes near the top of its head seemed to be constantly peering back at us whenever it faced us. But the bird wasn't watching us. It was, in fact, likely unaware of our presence. Instead it focused entirely on pulling worms from the soft earth. An American woodcock typically consumes its entire weight in worms daily. Worms, in fact, constitute up to 90 percent of a woodcock's diet; the rest comes from grubs, insect larvae, snails, and the like. Each day after the bird finished feeding, it returned to its boardwalk perch and settled down again in the sun to digest its meal.

Unfortunately, woodcock are declining in many areas. Habitat loss is the prime cause of the decline. Woodcock do not fare well in climax forests, requiring instead young woodlands or thickets with adjacent clearings or meadows. These fascinating birds are also adversely affected by excessive depredation of their eggs and young by raccoons, domestic cats, free-ranging dogs, and other predators whose populations are expanding.

On our sanctuary for songbirds, however, the woodcock population is growing. Habitat provided for other species serve these shorebirds well, and protection from predators allows the nests to survive and the young to thrive. Every spring and early summer several males display in our meadows as the sun makes its exit for the day.

When he lived in our motor home, Jeff and I spent many evenings at the edge of our meadow where we watched a displaying male. Just after dusk the bird would sit on the ground in the open field uttering a nasal "peent." One evening we were close enough to hear a surprising "hiccup" before the peent that neither of us had ever heard. The bird would then pause for a moment, turn ninety degrees, and repeat his hiccup and peent. After completing the circle, he began his courtship "sky dance" flight by spiraling up into the air. During his ascent, flight feathers produced a series of low trills, and then as he zigzagged earthward—much like a falling leaf—he whistled chirping sounds. Back on the ground, he started the process over again, continuing this elaborate courtship display for an hour or more in his nightly efforts to attract a mate.

When a woodcock male is successful, a female comes into his territory just long enough to mate with him. Then she will leave to lay her eggs in a "scrape," often at the edge of a woods, that she lines with dead leaves or other debris. While there was no way for us to know, this displaying male may have been accepted by the female along our back trail. If so, he would not have joined her to help with family duties. She would have incubated her eggs alone. Her hatchlings would have appeared after about three weeks and would have been able to follow her around in search of food almost immediately after they emerged from their shells.

Woodcock, sometimes called timberdoodles and a variety of other colorful names by hunters and old-timers, would never have inspired us to purchase our property, but we're happy they're around. They are a welcome addition. Because they have been so successful here, we expect to see their numbers grow until our sanctuary reaches the limit of its woodcock carrying capacity.

11

A Very Bumpy Night

The year we decided to open our home at Charter Sanctuary to paying guests was one of the hottest on record. That did not bode well for two people and two furry animals that had to spend many of their nights in a thinly insulated motor home while the guests slept in the house. During the day the blistering sun baked our RV and by early evening the interior temperature was often a hundred degrees or more. And we had no air conditioning in our motor home—or, rather, we had two roof units but neither worked. Although nights generally tend to be comfortable in this part of the country, that year they were like those of my childhood in southern Illinois—which is to say, they were miserable.

One evening in July when Jimmy, our two cats, and I moved into the rig, it was well over a hundred degrees inside. He had put a couple of fans in the windows earlier in the day in an effort to draw in fresh outside air, which was a relatively balmy ninety-five degrees. It hardly mattered—it was nearly as miserable outside as it was inside. Within an hour after we turned in, it started to rain. We closed the windows and the ovenlike interior of our motor home immediately transformed into a sauna. We both drifted in and out of sleep—mostly out; it was simply too hot to sleep. After a while the rain stopped and we opened the windows again. But the shower brought no relief. The air still felt like it was coming from a furnace, and it was heavily laden with moisture.

About two o'clock in the morning, the distant roar of a savage wind dragged us from our fitful slumber. Lightening strikes behind the squall line illuminated the downward curl of a menacing front bearing down from the west. We rose from our damp sheets and waited for the terrifying roar to reach us. It was, it seemed, a very long time before the tempest arrived. When it did, our rig rocked violently. Too nervous to sit, I paced the floor, waiting for the wicked wind from the west to carry us into the Land of Oz.

"Snap!" a tree went down nearby. "Snap! Snap!" Two more followed and another went down seconds later. Hailstones pounded the roof, and as another tree snapped, I lost count of the number of crashing trees. A lightening bolt struck nearby, so close that we could hear the "snik" as the charge found its way back down from the cloud. A second bolt exposed the horror outdoors—trees were bent nearly double, and the willows in the wetland lay as flat as if a giant hand had pressed them down.

Our skittish cat, Tashi, frantically wedged herself between the sofa and the wall in an attempt to escape the terrifying din. Amanda curled up half under a pillow on the sofa. The power failed, and Jimmy asked whether I would be less anxious in the house. I said that even if I would be, nothing would entice me out into the fury.

At the height of the storm, a light inexplicably went on in one of the vehicles in our driveway. Minutes later, a single light appeared inside the house, made its way first past the window next to my desk, then across the front door and into the dining room. There it paused before retracing its path. It vanished

briefly and then, ghostlike, it wandered through again.

When the winds finally abated, cooler air flowed through the window and we crawled back to bed. But I couldn't sleep. I lay in the quiet dark, wondering about the effect on our nesting birds. It was height of the breeding season. How many nests or eggs or nestlings were tossed from their trees in this violence?

Finally I drifted off into a fitful slumber but was awakened soon after dawn the next morning by the distress call of a robin. I pulled on my clothes and went out to find half a dozen aspens in a stand between the house and the barn broken in the middle. The riparian zone along a small creek that comes in from the west side of the meadow had suffered worse damage; there a dozen or more trees had gone down in the night. The robin was calling near a downed tree that had barely missed falling on the footbridge across the creek. I searched for the bird's nest but never found it. It was undoubtedly buried under the tangle of leaves and branches on the ground.

Inside the house, Jimmy was preparing breakfast for our guests, who were all up in spite of the early hour. One of the women explained the light roaming through the house during the storm. She said that her husband saw a ropelike funnel twisting across the landscape north of the house. Fearing the worst, he went to their car for a flashlight and his cell phone. While the storm raged around us, he wandered through the house with his flashlight in one hand and the cell phone in the other, searching for a way to our basement. Finding none (we don't have a basement), he then searched for the safest place to hunker down in case the roof was ripped off the house or the walls came crashing down around him. He finally decided the shower in their room would probably offer the most protection and tried to get her to go inside with him. She refused. She was not afraid, she said.

He was unapologetic.

"It was a very scary storm," he said.

"It certainly was scary," I agreed.

During my childhood, I learned firsthand about tornadoes. The winds raging outside in the night certainly had the sound of a tornado. But tornadoes are rare in our county because, we have been told, the lake surrounding us acts like a "weather fence" that breaks up violent weather before it reaches us. Moreover, the monster in the night hung around longer than any tornado in my memory. We also learned that the same wind had leveled 140,000 acres of woodlands in Minnesota.

While the storm had terrorized locals and caused a power outage, it had damaged only a few buildings. Trees were down everywhere. An enormous old maple had crashed over the state highway that runs up the edge of our peninsula and landed on the hood of a car driven by the brother of one of my coworkers. The car suffered considerable damage, but the driver escaped unhurt.

As for our birds, except for the robin whose nest apparently went down under the tree, we found no evidence of other losses. The season progressed with all of our known nesters carrying out their respective duties.

And the robin? When she could not locate her first nest, she immediately began again. Five weeks later, she brought her brood into the yard to search for worms.

12

Habitat by Fire

If "music is the speech of angels," as Scottish essayist Thomas Carlyle said, the joyous song of a bobolink rising over an otherwise silent meadow must be the voice of the archangel. Few other sounds lift the soul to such lofty heights as the effervescent tinkling of this small black bird. Many years ago the lyrical song of a bobolink prompted a child, hearing it for the first time, to ask his mother what made the bird sing so sweetly. Was it, the child wanted to know, because it ate flowers?

Bobolinks breed in meadows and fallow fields across southern Canada and down through about the northern half of our country. Marathon migrants, they travel all the way to Argentina's grassy pampas for the winter. In late summer and early fall they gather in great flocks in the southeastern states before heading to their wintering grounds. A tendency to gobble down grain to pack on weight earned them the nickname "butterbirds" in these states.

The male's ebony breeding plumage is broken by a soft yellow nape and white lower back, rump, and shoulders. It is an easy bird to find in the proper habitat—a large field or grassy meadow—where the reedy, ebullient notes of singing males can be heard in early summer. Possessed of a distinctive flight pattern, the bobolink moves through the air with its relatively long wings cupped downward. When ready to land, it flutters gracefully to a perch in the middle of the field.

Ground nesters, these handsome birds prefer damp meadows with dense grassy growth. When damp meadows are in short supply, they will accept drier, upland fallow fields. At one time they also nested successfully in hayfields. Although they still make the attempt, more often than not those nests fail. Today's farming practices require an earlier cutting of hay, a practice that frequently grinds up nestlings in the process.

When we bought our land Jimmy and I knew that bobolinks were declining. It was a decline that began nearly a century ago. The birds have a taste for rice, and when their enormous migrating flocks stripped rice fields at the dawn of the twentieth century, farmers reacted by killing them by the tens of thousands. In one year alone, more than seven hundred thousand bobolinks were reportedly shipped from a single South Carolina town for the bounty they would bring. As the century progressed, a series of Migratory Bird Acts halted the wanton destruction of bobolinks as well as many other birds. But some species never recovered. Bobolinks are one. Their decline continued after legislative protection because of vanishing habitat. They are losing ground across the continent and are now completely absent from New England, where they were once common.

But we didn't know the extent of the problem until Chip Francke walked the property with us. Chip, an authority on birds and their habitat needs, was the education director for the Leelanau Conservancy at the time. Because we had always intended to will the property to the Conservancy, we invited Chip and Conservancy Director Brian Price to walk the land with us soon after we bought it. The four of us waded through knee-deep snow into the woods and over the contours of the property to discuss its value to the birds of the area. When we reached the meadow, I said that we intended to let some of the open areas follow the natural successional stages from meadow through thicket to forest. We would retain part of the open uplands, but we wanted more woods. Chip immediately challenged our plan.

"You should keep the upland meadows open," he said. "That type of habitat is vanishing at a faster rate than any other kind all across the country."

When most of us visualize habitat loss, we typically think of wetlands being filled or old growth woodlands falling to the ax. Few imagine that abandoned, weedy fields are in danger of disappearing from our landscape. But the fact is that fields that either are not under cultivation or used for pasture are typically allowed to become overgrown. Eventually woody pioneer species like pin cherries replace grasses, weeds, and wildflowers. Those plants, in turn, are replaced by trees. Climax forests, dominated by maple and beech trees in Michigan, are the ultimate result.

These old forests are beautiful in their own right and provide homes for a number of specialized species that will not nest anywhere else. However, when we set out to preserve habitat, we should keep in mind that many more species require these fallow fields for survival.

Bobolinks depend on such habitat. Once enough shrubs and small trees overtake a field, the birds leave to find more suitable sites. Increasingly, no such sites are available. Upland nesters in our area also include eastern meadowlarks, grasshopper sparrows, vesper sparrows, upland sandpipers, dickcissels, and savannah sparrows. Woodcock need open meadows for "sky dance" courtship rituals. Numerous raptors, including snowy owls, forage over such fields.

We felt certain that bobolinks, as well as some of the other upland species, would eventually find their way to the thirty acres of meadow included in our land. The summer after we bought it, however, nothing nested in our fields. The farmer who owned it before us had planted rye the fall before it became ours. That first year the meadow produced a great crop of rye, but no upland birds. The second year was different. Eastern meadowlarks arrived in March and set up territories. Chip heard a horned lark and said that it might nest here— although we never found evidence of that. Vesper and savannah sparrows followed the meadowlarks. Finally, early in May of that second year, four bobolink males settled down in a damp swale that runs through the western side of our meadow. Because male bobolinks mate with more than one female, an undetermined number of females soon joined the males. Every year since, we have had bobolinks in increasing numbers. As the swale reached its carrying capacity, other pairs moved to higher ground. Within six years they were nesting above the garden.

By the time the birds were nesting above the garden, our fields had begun the forest succession process. In order to maintain the habitat required by our birds, the natural progression must be interrupted on a regular basis either by cutting or burning to eliminate emerging trees and shrubs. A visiting botanist recommended burning, which he thought might have the effect of killing off the alien species and encouraging native grasses to grow again in their place. Burning a field that ends just across a narrow drive from the house is a terrifying thought to a couple that once lost everything in a fire.

It helped that the local volunteer fire department agreed to do the burn as a training exercise. I had insisted on a fall burn so as not to interrupt summer's nesters. Unwilling to take on such a project without an explicit okay from the insurance company that had been so good to us after our disastrous fire, I contacted our agent. He was naturally reluctant to have us even consider such a thing. I explained that it was crucial to our bobolinks.

He argued; I pressed for approval.

Frustrated, he finally asked, "Which would you rather have, your bobolinks or your home?"

"Which would you rather have," I shot back, "your son or your daughter?"

He accepted that comparison, if a bit reluctantly, called our company, and explained the situation. To everyone's

surprise the company said we could do it so long as all the permits were in place and the fire department was involved. So the date was set. In the meantime I was a basket case. The field was covered with a thick layer of dead weeds and grasses. It was, in other words, full of fuel. I worried that the burn might get out of hand. One devastating fire is enough in anyone's lifetime.

On a Sunday morning late in October, the township's big pumper truck turned down our drive. Jimmy's nephew, Greg, was driving.

"Where do you want us to burn?" he asked.

Three of the firemen headed into the field; one poured lighter fuel on the dead vegetation and struck a match. A breeze blew out of the northwest—in the direction of the house, causing my anxiety level to ratchet up a couple of notches. I held my breath, waiting for the dead grasses to ignite flames that would race toward the house. Instead of catching, the flame sputtered and went out. The fireman tried again, and again the flame sputtered briefly before going out. They moved to another section and tried again with the same result. For more than forty-five minutes they tried to ignite one or another part of the field, but the fire never caught.

As it turned out, I had worried about the wrong result. An early morning drizzle drowned our plans. After failing to start the fire that I both wanted and feared, the firemen packed up and left.

"Don't worry, Kay," the chief said. "We'll get it for you."

We haven't gotten it yet. Another nesting season will soon be upon us, so we will have to wait until at least fall before we try again. Each year the vegetation is denser, generating more fuel and increasing the potential for disaster. But if I want to continue to hear the songs I most associate with angels, we must watch the field burn.

13

STARLING WARS

In 1890, sixty European starlings were released in New York's Central Park. Another forty were added the following year. Aggressive, opportunistic, and exceedingly prolific, those few birds grew to become hundreds and those, in turn, became thousands. Then there were millions. Today European starlings are one of the most common birds in North America. They blanket the continent.

A European starling dressed in its breeding plumage is a handsome bird sporting a bright yellow bill and iridescent feathers. Outside the breeding season its feathers are peppered with white speckles. The word *starling* means "little star" and derives from the bird's spangled appearance. But this chunky bird with a short tail is unwelcome in most quarters. Fruit farmers hate starlings. One year a local vintner lost his entire crop to great flocks of grape-eating invaders.

This species is the best example of the folly of bringing

foreign flora and fauna into the country. The impact of starlings on a number of native species has been devastating; they are responsible for the decline of any number of cavity-nesting North American birds. Among them are bluebirds. A starling will kill a brooding bluebird hen by entering her nest cavity and mantling her with its wings so that she can't escape. Then, with a single fatal blow, the starling drives its bill through her skull. If there are any chicks, they meet the same terrible fate.

After our barn was rebuilt, Jimmy put together a nest box for northern flickers and mounted it under the roof peak. A pair of flickers promptly moved in. My desk sits next to a window with a view across our yard to the barn and the flicker box. Working at my desk one afternoon, I looked out to see a starling sitting on the edge of the roof. Then, as I watched in horror, he entered the box, drove the flicker out, and began battering him. I raced outdoors to intervene and the two birds flew off in different directions. The flicker did not return; the starling did and moved in with his mate.

That same spring, starlings kicked wood ducks out of the box we had put up in our wetland for them, and they drove American kestrels from a kestrel box. They also drove another pair of flickers from a natural cavity high in a dead tree next to the creek in our woods. I happened to be in the vicinity for the last debacle. With me was artist and naturalist Tom Ford, who was identifying some of our woodland plants when the most horrible screams shattered the air. Tom is a lifelong resident of our county and knows virtually every plant, animal, bird, reptile, and insect in it. But he did not know what was responsible for the terrifying cries. We hurried in the direction of the ruckus and found a pair of starlings attacking the nesting flickers. The helpless flickers were once again driven from their nest site. After they were gone, we discovered the broken shells of four pure white eggs littering the ground underneath.

Thus began the starling wars.

I went to work with the pellet gun to rid our place of the avian enemy. It wasn't easy; starlings are extremely intelligent and wary creatures. For three weeks I tried to connect with one of the birds living in the nest on the barn, and for three weeks

I failed. Finally, using our car as a blind, I succeeded.

During one of my interviews with Frank Zuern about the bluebird house he developed, the subject of starlings came up. Zuern said that if you broke the wings on a dead starling and hung it upside down near the nest box, its mate would abandon the box and others of its kind would avoid it. We followed his advice and hung the bird I had dispatched with the pellet gun by its feet from the eave of the barn. It worked, and, at least for the rest of that summer, starlings stayed away from our barn.

But a dead bird hanging prominently from a building wasn't exactly the best face to present to visitors who came to our bird sanctuary for walks or habitat classes. Each new group brought questions or comments.

"I thought this place was a safe haven for birds," was the most common remark.

We assured our visitors that it was a safe haven, but not for all birds. Rather, it was specifically established for songbirds whose numbers are declining. We described the destructive behavior of nesting starlings and explained how that behavior is at least partly responsible for the decline of bluebirds and other cavity nesters across the country. We told them that an ornithologist from New Mexico had informed us during a visit to our sanctuary that starlings are responsible for the eradication of red-headed woodpeckers in his state. Red-headed woodpeckers are declining in Michigan, and starlings are at least partly to blame. We added that we would not have poured all of our earthly resources into a sanctuary to assist starlings. These birds need no help; they will undoubtedly flourish long after the rest of us are nothing but faint memories on the planet. All of our visitors accepted our explanation about the starling dangling upside down from our barn eave.

When the birds returned the next nesting season, the battle resumed. We read that we could discourage starlings by waiting until later in the season to put up nest boxes, but that didn't work. Then we read that starlings preferred dark nest sites and that painting the insides of nest boxes white would discourage them. It doesn't. In the hope of providing a site for something other than starlings, we mounted a box deep within the branches of a dense conifer, hoping that the European invaders wouldn't find it. That failed as well; starlings discovered and claimed the box. We tried another tack—waiting until their nest was complete and then removing nest material. The starlings began rebuilding as soon as we walked away from the box. We waited until we knew they had eggs inside and then stuffed the hole with newspapers; they promptly pulled the stuffing back out. We removed the eggs. They laid more.

We finally withdrew from the field of battle and removed all nest boxes except the bluebird/tree swallow boxes in our upland meadow. Starlings can't use these boxes because the entrance hole on that design is too small to allow them entry.

The month after we opened our B&B, a pair of great crested flycatchers began calling from our woods. We decided to try one last time to provide a site for one of our natives. We had neither seen nor heard starlings for more than a month. One morning a few weeks later, I was picking strawberries near the box put up for the flycatchers and saw a starling carry a bill full of insects to it. Seized by the fury of the defeated, I grabbed the garden hose, carried it to the base of the post, turned the water on full blast, and managed to wrangle the end up into the box, which was about ten feet off the ground. I left it there until water flowed from all sides, believing I had drowned its contents.

I hadn't. The next morning, the parent was back carrying food into the box. By afternoon, the young had fledged.

Local farmers say that winning the starling war is impossible, but I refuse to accept defeat. I am determined to outwit the invaders so that someday, native cavity nesters who choose Charter Sanctuary as their breeding site will nest here without molestation.

14

FOUNDLINGS

When we bought our land people often asked whether we planned to include wildlife rehabilitation in our efforts. We assured them that we were not going to accept orphaned birds to care for; managing forty-seven acres for migrating and nesting birds would be a full-time job in itself. There were trees to plant, trails to cut, nest boxes to build and maintain. We wanted to develop a hummingbird garden. There was also, of course, the habitat classes I wanted to teach and the mundane business of earning our own keep.

But the best-laid plans of mice and dedicated birders can be sidetracked by unforeseen events. Thus a quick noontime trip to the mall ultimately led us into the world of rehabilitation. We are not shoppers and almost never go to either of the two big malls in the nearby town of Traverse City, but early in the summer after we moved into our home, I stopped at the larger of the malls for some necessary item. As I returned to my car, five tiny ducklings scrambled across the parking lot in my direction. A ring-billed gull called from a nearby light standard. Gulls eat ducklings, and the ring-billed was no doubt waiting for a chance to snag an easy meal.

I looked around for their mother, who should have been with them, but there was no hen in sight. Instead another two ducklings streaked across the pavement, running my way. Four more scurried along behind. I scooped up the first five and shouted at the shopper who had followed me out of the store to stop the others. She looked at me as if I'd asked her to pick up a live grenade and hurried to her car. A mall security guard came around the corner, saw my dilemma, and helped me gather up the tiny yellow-and-brown creatures. Then someone driving by saw our struggle to hang onto eleven ducklings and stopped to offer us a cardboard box.

The security guard asked me what these ducklings were doing running around a vast concrete parking lot without their mother.

"She's either injured or dead," I said. "Otherwise she wouldn't have let them out of her sight."

He went to the intersection that lay in the direction they had come from and found his answer—their mother, a mallard hen, was dead. A car had hit her. When he returned, he was saddened by what he had seen, and by its implications. He was also furious at the driver who had done the deed and wished aloud that he could get his hands on the culprit.

"What on earth are we going to do with them?" he asked.

"I'm taking them home," I said. "My husband and I have the perfect place for them."

We put them in the box, and I made the long drive home serenaded by eleven peeping ducklings. With the help of a local bird rehabilitation specialist, we secured the necessary permit, and Jimmy built a cage for them. Five of them promptly died. Two more expired before they were grown, which, we were assured by a local expert, was no reflection on the kind of care we had provided.

We thought we knew mallards fairly well, but we learned a great deal about these handsome waterfowl during the time we served as their surrogate parents. One thing we were surprised to discover was that they had distinct personalities. The brightest youngster was also the most gregarious. When we cleaned their swimming pool, he was always first into the water, shooting around underneath like a seal. One of the ducklings was a bit of a slow learner; he was shyer and never figured out how to get out of the cage when we opened it in the morning. Each day when I opened the door, his three nest mates would promptly waddle out, and he would walk back and forth on the inside fussing at them. Then I'd gently prod him in the direction of the door so that he could join the others for a meal and a swim.

Although we provided the four young birds with a commercial food developed specifically for ducks, we were not surprised that from the very first day they were in our care they supplemented their domestic diet with whatever natural food they were able to catch or find. We did not, however, expect them to sift through the mud with their bills—like we've seen shovelers do—in search of tender roots. And we never would have guessed that they would extract plump earthworms from soft dirt or that they might snap up flying insects that happened by within range. Watching a tiny duckling act like a flycatcher is a funny sight indeed.

Like all youngsters, they grew up too quickly. To give them their best chance of surviving in the wild, we weren't planning to release them until they were ready to fly. They soon outgrew their cage and Jimmy built them a pen in the yard. We used a child's swimming pool for their pond, which we had to clean several times a day to eliminate the droppings. Whenever we took the hose into their pen to refill their pond, they nipped at the stream of fresh water. A freshly cleaned pool always meant an immediate and exuberant dip—with our head of the class leading the way. At night we hustled them back into their cage for protection from coyotes, which visit nightly.

Because of an illness in the family, I had to leave the state just as our adoptees' flight feathers were growing in. I wanted very much to see them set out on their own, but feared they would be ready to leave before I was able to return. Happily, they were not. When I got back home, our full-grown and fully feathered ducks were still inside their large fenced pen, but they were restless. Late in the day of my return, our most precocious duck eyed the world beyond his pen with agitated interest.

These were wild creatures, and we did not want to make pets of them. I did, however, develop a tremendous affection for them while they were under our care. While we did not give them names, I did allow myself the luxury of calling them our "duckies."

Our duckies had been protected and cared for all their young lives and had absolutely no street smarts about how to survive in the wild and woolly world outside their pen. While much is instinctive, their mother undoubtedly would have taught them some things that we could not. So even though it appeared they were ready to leave when I got back from my trip late one afternoon, we decided to hold them for one more night. A morning release seemed prudent.

Our smart duck had other ideas. As dusk settled over the property we heard a single loud, "Quack!" We went outside to find him standing in the middle of the driveway waiting for his mates to join him. We herded him back into the pen and shut him inside with his nest mates.

The next morning we opened the cage, peeled the fence back from the pen, and released them. They lifted into the air immediately. I felt a twinge of sadness as they flew out of the yard. Jimmy must have felt the same way.

"Well, I guess they're gone," he said wistfully as they winged their way over the house.

"I guess they are," I agreed.

Not quite. They circled the property once and came back. One landed behind the barn, two others came down in the cattails, and our little slow learner nearly hit the house. After they found their way back to the yard, they waddled into their then open-sided pen and settled down for a long rest. Later in the day they took off again, circling the property twice before landing helter-skelter as before and returning to their pen. In the evening, they left and didn't return. Sunrise found them back in their pen for a bite of Duck Grower and another long nap in the shade.

During the following week, they returned alone, by twos, or all together for various parts of the day. At night they always left again. The last time they headed out, they flew straight north where a little pond is nestled in the trees. We went to check on them only once. A week after they left for good, we walked over to the pond with our binoculars. Four ducks were at the far end. To determine if they were our duckies, I called them as I always had when I took their food out to them in the pen. They immediately began to swim in our direction, but we did not wait for them. Satisfied that they were taking care of themselves in the wild with no help from us, we left them alone. We walked back to the house with the happy knowledge that they were grown and healthy and in their element, far from the parking lot where they were found and the busy road that took their mother's life.

Friends who got to know our ducks often ask whether we have ever seen them since that first year. We don't know. Certainly we often see mallards in the small open pools in our wetland, but we have no idea whether any of them are from the four that grew up here. Because mallards can live ten or more years in the wild, there is a good possibility that occasionally one of these birds comes by for a visit. Two weekend guests at our B&B spotted a hen and half a dozen ducklings waddling through our yard and declared that the mother duck must have been one of ours. She just seemed to fit here, they decided. We couldn't argue otherwise.

15

A FINE KETTLE OF HAWKS

One afternoon in mid-August, while waiting in town for my husband, I killed time with a favorite pastime—sky watching. Anything can appear overhead in late summer, from chittering chimney swifts to soaring sandhill cranes. On this particular day, I was especially fortunate—soaring overhead was an incredible phenomenon known as a kettle of hawks.

Groups of birds are referred to in a number of ways depending on which species is being discussed and whether they are on the ground or in the air. While a handful of quail scurrying into a thorny tangle is a covey, the same number of young chickens escaping danger is a clutch or brood. A bunch of ducks on the wing is a flock, but when they land on water and float in close proximity, they become a raft. To my grandmother, and likely everyone else's, a flock of geese in the farmyard was a gaggle. A flight of woodcock was once known as a fall, an appropriate name as anyone can attest who has watched them drop from the sky to an upland thicket.

Then there is the name for an aerial whirlpool of hawks, swirling over the landscape as they migrate. At times the hawks in such a vortex will number in the thousands. This grand grouping of birds is known as a kettle. Most birds of prey take advantage of rising thermals of air warmed over sun-heated landmasses, both to hunt and to migrate. One bird hunting or two birds moving along a column of warmed air is simply one or two birds soaring within a thermal. But when raptors use thermals in numbers, they are said to be "kettling."

I have long understood the term "kettle" to have originated when someone, years ago, watching a mass of birds soaring up a thermal was reminded of a kettle of boiling water. Recently, however, Dr. Keith Bildstein, director of research and education at Pennsylvania's Hawk Mountain Sanctuary, told me during a telephone interview that the word actually evolved in the region surrounding the sanctuary. He said that the valley east of the sanctuary was settled by German immigrants, who called the rather round-bottomed valleys *kessels*, which means "kettles" in English. As early hawkwatchers observed migrating raptors ride thermals up from those depressions, they first said, "The hawks are in the kettles again." That evolved to "The hawks are kettling," which ultimately became "a kettle of hawks."

Migrating raptors—and other families like cranes and pelicans—take advantage of rising columns of warmed air. The birds consistently catch those thermals that move in the direction they are heading: north in spring and south in late summer and early fall. They ride up thermals and, on reaching the top—which can be thousands of feet in the air—string out and glide down to the base of the next column of rising warm air. Then they ride the next thermal up in the same way and begin again. They don't have to flap their wings, either on the way up the thermal or as they glide down to the next one. By simply spreading their wings and balancing on the draft, much as a surfer does on a wave, they allow the invisible current to take them as far as it goes. It is a very energy-efficient way of travel.

More than a hundred hawks soared up the rising column

of air that morning in August. Although it was directly overhead when I first discovered it, it was drifting slowly to the southeast. It carried a mixed bag of birds as it moved: red-tailed, sharp-shinned, Cooper's, and broad-winged hawks rode up the rising current on open wings. Another broad-winged hawk streamed in from the north to take advantage of the invisible escalator. I looked behind the bird and saw still more hawks following, first a red-tail, another broad-wing, and then a sharpie. Then multiple birds began streaming into the thermal—all moving at an incredible speed considering that there wasn't a single wing beat among them.

I watched as the birds circled the thermal, climbing ever higher into the sky. The broad-wing at the top of the kettle was so far up that it was nearly out of sight, yet it still was soaring higher. I'd never seen more than a dozen or so birds in a kettle before, nor had I ever seen the dynamics of birds moving in to grab a thermal, riding to the top, and then spilling over on a glide path for the next column of rising air. It was a thrilling sight.

Kettling occurs mostly where raptors are concentrated—either beside a barrier like the Great Lakes or along a mountain range where thermals are abundant. One favorite hawkwatching site is Michigan's Whitefish Point along Lake Superior's southern shore. But there are others: Hawk Mountain Sanctuary is the best known, and Cape May, New Jersey, is also good.

The greatest concentration of hawks, however, occurs just west of Corpus Christi, Texas, where the shoreline of the Gulf of Mexico makes a sweeping curve and turns nearly straight south. Known as the Coastal Bend, this area concentrates hawks migrating south across the continent. Most birds are reluctant to head over water, and the Gulf of Mexico is a formidable barrier to hawks moving southward from throughout the eastern half of the continent. When hawks reach the coasts of Georgia, Alabama, Mississippi, and Louisiana, they swing west toward the Coastal Bend and are met by another mass of birds moving down from the heartland. At the right time, ten thousand or more individual birds can be seen in fantastic kettles. While kettles at other sites are typically mixed and may include anything from tiny American kestrels to both bald and golden eagles, the vast majority of birds in the great kettles of the Coastal Bend are broad-winged hawks headed to winter in South America.

About ten miles west of downtown Corpus Christi is a small park officially named Hazel Bazemore County Park. Birders know it simply as Hazel Bazemore. Within the park boundaries is a hill that rises eighty-five feet above sea level—merely a bump in the landscape to anyone from a mountainous state. But within the broad, coastal plains of Texas, this little hill— the highest in four counties—provides hawk watchers with just enough elevation to count hawks in kettles over a fairly wide area. For a few days in the last week of September—if conditions are right—hawkwatchers on this hill will count some one hundred thousand to three hundred thousand hawks a day. Perhaps the largest sustained concentration of hawks ever seen occurred from August 15 through November 15, 1998, when nearly a million hawks were counted.

The largest single kettle ever documented was recorded by hawk counter Joel Simon and his team on September 27, 1997. On that memorable day, Simon reported seventy-six thousand hawks in a single kettle. "This massive kettle was first spotted well out to the horizon, and the stream that came out of the top was more like a river," he said. "It varied from forty to eighty hawks wide and took twenty-two minutes to pass the count point."

To the unskilled eye, it must have looked like a slow-moving tornado or whirling dervish. By comparison, the kettle I saw in Leelanau County was a petite ballet in the sky—a gentle tease for a pair of eyes hungry for the spectacular sight of thousands of hawks spiraling up the currents as they make their way from one continent to another.

16

CHICKADEE ROYALTY

Jeff asked me during his first visit to our property, "If you had to choose one kind of bird to watch for the rest of your life and give up all the others, which one would you pick?"

"Chickadees," I said without hesitation.

He agreed.

Spread across the continent, chickadees include the blacked-capped species of the northern states and the Carolina species of the South, as well as boreal, mountain, chestnut-backed, and Mexican species. Jeff and I aren't alone. Chickadees are the favorite of many people. Why would two people who spend a good deal of time watching birds put this rather common bird at the top of their lists? I think it's this bird's friendly, gregarious personality that attracts us. Chickadees seem to have a cheerful joie de vivre as they go about their daily affairs. If they were human, we'd say they had plenty of charisma, and maybe even a little chutzpah.

But those aren't the only traits that attract people to chickadees. We also like them for their sense of fair play. When a flock of chickadees comes to a feeder, the birds approach one at a time, taking only a seed or two from the tray. Then each, in turn, flies up to a nearby branch to eat the seed before returning for another. The appearance of equality, however, is deceiving. Studies of black-capped chickadees have revealed a firm social structure that prevents them from approaching feeders as equals. Instead, the order in which they come is rigidly prescribed.

Chickadees form breeding flocks of several pairs, and every individual within those pairs usually forms a lifelong bond with its mate. There are also "floaters," individuals that drift back and forth between several breeding flocks in an area. Within the breeding flock there is a permanent hierarchy, at the top of which is the dominant, or alpha, pair. Every other pair, as well as the floaters, defers to the dominant pair.

The alpha male is like a king, taking his food before any of the others when the flock visits a feeder. He is followed first by his mate, then by others in the flock, each in its hierarchical turn. Like royalty, the alpha pair retains its position as long as they live. Floaters have their own hierarchy, with a dominant individual at the top. They don't form pair bonds, however, and they don't mate until they join the breeding flock, which they often do to fill the place of a lost bird. If the flock's alpha male is lost, for example, the highest-ranking floating male usually takes its place.

Black-capped chickadees were the first birds to appear when we put up our feeders. Almost immediately one member of the flock took to us in a personal way. He beat a path to our feeders every time we went out to refill them, even if plenty of seed remained inside. Early on he landed on Jimmy's hand as he was refilling a feeder one morning. Jimmy offered seeds from his palm and the chickadee promptly selected one. For some unknown reason, this little guy developed an immediate affinity for us, and from that day on, he regularly took seed from our hands regardless of whether or not there was seed in the feeders.

He followed both of us whenever we worked in the yard, settling on a branch near us and emitting his *dee-dee-dee* call, begging for food. In order to accommodate this little mooch, we took to stuffing a handful of sunflower seeds in our pockets on the way out the door. And when we returned from our winter hiatus in the Southwest, he was always perched on a prominent branch, begging for seed as soon as we exited our motor home.

One day he scared the wits out of me by landing on the

bill of my cap just as I leveled the sights of my air gun on a starling and pulled the trigger. Our feathered friend could easily have flown into the line of fire at precisely the wrong moment, so after that heart-stopping experience, I was doubly vigilant during armed skirmishes with the exotic black birds.

Chickadees regularly entertained me during slow times at the lighthouse gift shop. Occasionally I would hear a *chip* from the open door. Early on I learned that the sound meant one of the black-capped little bandits was fluttering at a spider web stretched across the transom window. It would hover there, calling cheerfully as it raided insects caught in a spider's painstakingly crafted trap. The birds always continued these little forays until the web was scoured clean. I have since noticed that raiding spider webs is a relatively common chickadee behavior.

Charter Sanctuary was not established for black-capped chickadees. These ubiquitous characters thrive across much of the continent without any particular assistance from humans. We would have them no matter how much or little property we had. But our lives are certainly enriched by the presence of these delightful little birds and their carefully structured society.

17

KINGBIRD AT THE WINDOW

Beware the pronouncements of experts. If we had listened to a trained wildlife rehabilitation specialist, we would never have adopted a fledgling kingbird. And if we had not adopted this young bird, we would have missed one of the most exciting and satisfying experiences we've had on our sanctuary. The "expert" told us that orphaned songbirds couldn't be saved. She was wrong.

Early in August, I led a float boat tour for our Leelanau Conservancy. While we cruised slowly through a marvelous fen that is part of the Conservancy's holdings, one of the participants asked me about rehabilitating songbirds, and I offered up the doctrine according to our acquaintance. Dan and Lillian Mahanney were along on that trip. Lil, who is a rehabilitation specialist, gently contradicted me.

"I am raising an eastern kingbird right now," she said. "He was found in a cherry orchard during harvest when he was only a couple of days old."

Rehabbers, as they are called, worry about people taking young animals that appear to be without parents. Usually the parents of babies that seem to be orphaned are nearby but out of sight. For that reason, people are always advised to leave wild youngsters where they are for twenty-four hours. If the parents haven't returned by the next day, then measures can be taken to protect the abandoned youngster. Lil made sure the people on the boat understood that.

"The man who found the bird did the right thing," she said. "The nest had tumbled out of a tree, and when he found it, he put the tiny chick and his two mates back inside and placed the nest in the nearest tree. An hour or so later, he began to worry about the chicks and went back to check on them. He found the nest back on the ground, one of the birds dead and another gone. Only one bird was alive. Fearing that putting it back in the tree again would mean certain death, he brought it to us. That was nearly two weeks ago; our little hatchling is now fully feathered and ready to leave our care."

Two days later, Lil called and asked if she could bring her charge to our property for release. She learned during our boat trip that Jimmy and I had established our sanctuary for songbirds, and she hoped we would accept the kingbird since releasing him on their property was out of the question. Kingbirds need open space in which to forage for insects. The Mahanneys live in the woods—the wrong habitat.

I said that we'd be delighted to have him.

Jeff and his birder fiancée Becky were visiting that weekend. When I told them about the forthcoming release, Jeff said, "There's no better place for him. But he'll have to deal with the kingbirds that are already here. The first thing that will probably happen to him will be that your resident kingbirds will beat the stuffin' out of him."

Kingbirds get their names from the fact that they are extremely territorial during the nesting season and will drive off any avian interlopers, including hawks, herons, and members of their own kind that are not immediate family.

The Mahanneys arrived just before eight the following morning with a large birdcage resting on the back seat of their van. Inside the cage was a plump and curious, if slightly puzzled, young kingbird. Lil took the bird from the cage and held him up next to the long, narrow stand of pin cherries that runs between our home and the wetland. The bird immediately flew to the top of one of the trees. Lil coaxed him back down to a branch near her, fed him a handful of mealworms, passed me the small plastic can filled with the worms, and left.

Jeff's prediction was right. Before the Mahanneys were out of the drive, a resident kingbird attacked the startled fledgling and tried to drive him away. Our newcomer may have been young, but he had the right stuff. The young kingbird snapped his bill back at the aggressor and held his ground.

No one—including Lil, as this was the first kingbird she had raised—had any idea how quickly this bird would adapt to the outdoors, how much supplemental feeding he might need, or even if he would hang around. We chose the pin cherries for release because the fruit was ripe. The fledgling could rely at least partly on those cherries while he learned to hawk the flying insects that would become a major part of his diet if he were to survive. After his encounter with the attacking kingbird, our fledgling studied a cherry on one of the trees carefully. Then he snapped it off with his bill and swallowed it. It was the first time in this kingbird's young life that he had selected a bit of food on his own.

Jimmy and I had planned to take Jeff and Becky to an auction that day. Satisfied that the bird could manage on its own for at least a while, we left for our outing. We were away for nearly eight hours. On the way back, we speculated on how the kingbird had fared during our absence and discussed how we might offer him any supplements if they were needed. How, we wondered, would we get the worms Lil left up to the bird if he were high in the tree? We all assumed that the bird probably would not respond to any voice but Lil's since she was the only human that had fed him from the time he was rescued from the orchard. Therefore, we reasoned, we needed a way to transport the worms up to the bird.

Jeff's resourceful fiancée offered the best suggestion.

"Maybe if we nail a small can—like a tuna can—to the

end of a long stick and put the worms in the can, we would be able to hold it up high enough that he will come and eat from it," Becky said. But our concerns proved to be without foundation, and Becky's brilliant suggestion was unneccessary.

We returned to find a very hungry kingbird perched well up in a pin cherry. He was close to where he had been released and was making a very insistent begging sound. Jeff picked up a mealworm in his fingers and held it over his head. The bird immediately dropped to a low branch and snatched the wiggling worm. In quick succession, he ate twenty-five more, muttering—a little like a nursing infant—as he ate. He went back up for about ten minutes to digest his meal, then came back for more.

Later in the day, the bird moved to the southern edge of the pin cherries where he studied a goldfinch as it drank from the birdbath. After the finch left, the kingbird flew down to the birdbath and landed on its edge. Then he sat for a long time, eyeing the water and cocking his head first one way and then the other. Finally he dipped his bill into the water and took his first tentative drink.

Jeff fed him several times that day and when the kingbird came for his mealworms that evening, he landed on Jeff's arm. Night was closing in, the temperature was dropping, and this little creature was ready to settle down for a sleep. After eating, he snuggled against Jeff's chest, seeking in Jeff's woolly shirt the warmth he had been accustomed to after the sun went down.

"You're cold, aren't you?" Jeff said to him. And then to us, "I'm sure he wants to come inside."

But taking him inside would have required a birdcage, which we didn't have. We also knew that taking him indoors wouldn't be good in the long run. He was a late hatchling and had less than four weeks to finish growing up and to prepare for the long migration south. While he looked much like a fully grown kingbird, he was only two and a half weeks old. Having imprinted on humans, the kingbird looked to the one holding him for protection from the increasingly cold air.

"I'm sorry little guy...we can't take you in," Jeff said softly.

Then he urged him to fly into an overhead branch.

Even though it was early August, the mercury dropped into the low forties that night. Our innate sense of nurturing was enhanced by our affection for the baby bird—and by the fact that he so easily accepted our offerings. Each of us felt protective of him, so no one slept well. The next morning we were all up at dawn and found the kingbird begging fiercely from his treetop perch. This time he refused to descend to get his worms. He stayed in the top of the tree no matter how much coaxing we did. Then we saw the problem: another kingbird had come in to harass him. The older bird attacked, screeching and snapping. Our little guy snapped back, then dived into the safer interior of the tree branches. And there he sat, fussing for food. Finally the interloper left and the fledgling came down to be fed. He ate thirty worms as fast as Jeff could pick them out of the can. Within an hour he had feasted on more than fifty additional mealworms and snagged a couple of passing mosquitoes, bringing a cheer of approval from his human observers.

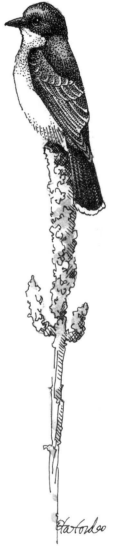

Eastern kingbirds are flycatchers, birds that primarily make their living catching insects on the wing. It was good to see that our foster bird at least had the right idea. Before noon that day, he greedily gobbled down another twenty-nine worms and snagged two more mosquitoes. Late in the afternoon, Becky was able to capture several houseflies. She put the flies in a jar in the fridge so they would be less active and then offered them to our feathered guest. Her treat went over very well.

I had my first experience feeding him that day. I will never forget how light he was when he landed on my hand, the feeling of his tiny claws pressing gently into the flesh on my fingers, or the way he muttered while he took the worms I offered.

We established a protocol. When he called for food, we would go out onto the deck off of our kitchen, which is about eight feet from the ground and within reach of the pin cherries where he had established his home base. If he was off in the northern end of the trees, we could call "kingbird!" and he would fly in to take his meal. One morning he added his own twist. When we didn't get out on the deck early enough to suit him, he perched just on the other side of the kitchen window where Jimmy sat with his coffee and nagged until my mate took the can of worms out to feed him.

We did not band him, never attempted to hold him, and always allowed him to come to us. We would take the worms from the little plastic can, place them in the palm of an outstretched hand, and wait for him to land on our fingers to pick them up. Sometimes he dallied in the tree, watching us from just out of our reach, and the worm would wriggle out of our palm and drop to the ground below the deck, providing the chickadees with a culinary windfall.

Toward the end of the first week, a cold front blew in from the northwest. I listened to the rain beat on the bedroom window through the night and wondered how the kingbird was faring. Lil worried about him, too, and called the next day to see how he had made out. Morning found him in his usual place in the cherry tree, begging away. He took thirty-two worms before hopping up to a higher branch where he sat to digest his meal.

The following day Jimmy had to go out of town. I had to work and would be away for ten hours. The kingbird hadn't gone more than eight hours without supplemental food since he'd been released. If the weather had been nicer, we wouldn't have been concerned, but it was a raw, stormy day with high winds. We thought he might need additional nourishment in order to stay warm, so our good friend—and birder—Pat Bussey offered to fill in for an afternoon feeding. When she arrived late in the day, the kingbird wolfed down thirty-one worms.

By the time I got off work, the winds had picked up and were at gale force. When I got home, he was voracious, perhaps because the high winds had prevented him from foraging, and he was undoubtedly burning a lot of fuel to stay warm. I fed him another thirty worms and realized that the can was virtually empty. I called the Mahanney's for more worms, but they weren't home. Several other calls also failed. Fearing I would run out completely, I followed Becky's example and captured a baker's dozen flies from the garage. Until that day, I never would have believed that I could capture one live fly, much less thirteen.

Dan and Lil had to replenish our worm supply a number of times while we cared for the bird. Once they left a can of wax worms—short, bloated grubs that look a bit like stunted white tomato worms. Lil had said that the bird didn't really like them much but would take them when he was exceptionally hungry. This was not a job for anyone squeamish about worms. But the evening of the storm, except for the few flies I was able to capture, there was nothing else to offer him. After the flies were gone, I served up the fat and squishy wax worms one by one. He took them like a kid devouring candy.

Our kingbird was increasingly able to care for himself, and he began to take more and more time to come down and feed. Sometimes he sat on a high branch and fussed for us to come up to him rather than flying down to us for his supplement. He weaned himself, coming for his last supplement two weeks to the day after he had been released. This time he came in the company of another kingbird, and there was no squawking and gnashing of bills. The new bird sat at a distance and watched the young bird come to my hand for the last of the nearly one thousand mealworms we'd fed him over the previous two weeks.

Over the next couple of weeks growing numbers of

kingbirds made their way down the peninsula, and I began to fear that without parents to show the way, ours wouldn't migrate as he must. One morning on my way to work I found a dead kingbird in the center of the road. A passing car had hit it—a reminder of the incredible challenges facing our bird. If he made it to the Gulf Coast without crashing into a vehicle, plate-glass window, or communication tower, he still faced that long trip across the Gulf of Mexico to the Yucatan Peninsula. Then he would continue his southward journey until he reached Peru or Bolivia. If he survived that, he would have to do it all again for the return trip in spring.

Migration is fraught with danger, but it is essential. Winter in Leelanau County was impossible for this Neotropical creature. I e-mailed Jeff about my concerns.

His response, "Tell that kingbird to get the hell out of Dodge!"

Labor Day came and went and he stayed. The middle of the month passed and he was still here. Then one morning he was gone. Although we were relieved that he finally started south, we missed hearing his persistent chatter from the perch on top of the pin cherry trees. Our yard seemed suddenly empty. Godspeed little bird, I thought. It's a long way to South America.

18

A Life Bird Makes
a House Call

In late August my sisters Vicki and Chris surprised us with a visit. I was thrilled at the prospect of showing them our part of the world, our home, and—best of all—the birds on our sanctuary.

They arrived late on Thursday afternoon, and after breakfast the next morning the three of us walked the property. As we hiked to the top of the hill beyond the wetland and stood where Jimmy and I had first looked at the land, I expressed a bit of regret that they couldn't have come in mid-June when nearly all our nesters would still have been around. By late August the breeding season was mostly behind us. Many migrating species were already gone. Grasshopper sparrows and warbling vireos had left a week earlier. Tree swallows had been gone for nearly two months. Although bobolinks were still around, the males had lost their distinctive breeding plumage and their songs no longer filled our fields.

Some birds remained on the property, however, and I was able to point out a few Charter Sanctuary species. A redstart family foraged alongside the trail where it curls into the woods, and when we reached the thicket at the edge of the woods, we kicked up a small covey of grouse. I told them about the family Fred Case and I had disturbed earlier in the year, and we wondered whether these might be the same birds.

The best find on our walk was the male indigo bunting singing from the top of a young elm tree at the bottom of the hill. It was a special thrill to find this bird. A month earlier the local power company brought in a huge machine to trim brush under the lines that run along the north side of our sanctuary. The machine digested everything in its path, including a bunting nest. Devastated at the destruction, I called the company and talked to the right-of-way maintenance manager. He was very responsive and came out the next day. I showed him a picture of the bird with the rich blue plumage and explained that a pair of these lovely finches had nested in the tangle of plants under his company's power line every year since we had bought this land. He expressed sadness over the loss and promised to never again order trimming along our property without contacting us first.

In the meantime, the buntings had found another spot to nest.

The next day Jimmy joined the three of us when we headed down to the town of Buckley, a little over an hour south of our home. I was scheduled to drive an enormous steam tractor—properly referred to as an antique steam traction engine—in an old engine show there.

The engine, a giant "40" made in 1911 by the Avery Company of Peoria, Illinois, was originally purchased by Nebraska rancher Edward McPherrin to facilitate work on his 6,400-acre ranch. Although it set him back a hefty $4,250, McPherrin abandoned this magnificent piece of equipment in a grove of trees after using it only briefly. There it remained for forty years. The rancher, and his sons after him, worked around it as though it didn't exist.

Hidden away in a vast ranch and virtually forgotten by its

owner, the Avery escaped the destiny of other great steamers. Some were worked to death while others were dispassionately dropped into swamps for road fill. Many went to feed the Second World War's voracious appetite for scrap metal. But this Avery survived. And it did so in remarkably good condition because it was deserted in a relatively dry part of the country. It is now an exquisitely preserved rarity, owned by Tom and Kathy Graham of East Jordan, Michigan.

Large steam traction engines were developed to bust up tough prairie sod in the heart of the country. This sod had roots that were as big as a man's thumb and reached down six feet into the earth. Horse teams of sixteen or more were not sturdy enough to pull a plow through the dense tangle of tough roots. And the first, relatively small steam traction engines—which were simply adaptations of stationary engines that had been used for thrashing wheat and ginning cotton—weren't much better. They broke down repeatedly under the strain. Elephant power was called for. Thus were born monsters like the Avery, capable of developing power that, translated into human terms, would enable an average man to lift a Jeep Cherokee on his outstretched palm. And thus the steam that had already changed the world of manufacturing was harnessed for agriculture, altering the face of the American farm forever.

I fell in love with the Graham's machine the year before while working on a piece about the Buckley Old Engine Show for a national magazine. After the article appeared, I wanted to write another that focused entirely on the Avery. When I talked to Tom about it, he offered to help in any way he could. One thing I asked for was a chance to drive his engine in order to get a feel for it. He agreed to that and so Jimmy, my sisters, and I arrived at the show in midmorning—in time for me to maneuver the Avery for the plowing demonstration.

Graham invited me to ride up the hill to the plow field on the back of the engine. I jumped on board and clasped the handhold with the casual assurance of a sailor who knows her sea legs won't fail her. As Tom opened the throttle, tremendous steam pressure rushed into the engine's two cylinders and fired up the pistons. Powerful vibrations racked the machine and shook the ground underneath. When he shifted into low gear, the behemoth, puffing a dense plume of dark smoke, lurched to a start and nearly threw me off the back. I tightened my grip as he steered away from the club's parade grounds and turned up the hill alongside the railroad track. We passed Jimmy and my sisters on the way up. They caught up with us and watched as I took the wheel for the length of the plowed field.

"I haven't seen you smile like that since I was a kid," Chrissy said when I dismounted from the giant.

She should have been with Jeff and me when we came across a short-eared owl roosting up on our hillside. Driving the Avery was a very exciting experience, but it didn't begin to compare with the thrill of finding this bird on our property.

Pat and Clay Sutton wrote in their book *How to Spot an Owl* that in order to find owls, one must spend a great many hours in the field, mostly without success. Our search for a glimpse of the short-eared owl proves the Suttons' point.

Short-eared owls are birds of open marshes, prairies, and

fields. They are crepuscular, meaning they hunt during the low light of dawn and dusk, and they can turn up virtually anywhere across the entire North American continent. These two facts should make them easier to locate than their nocturnal cousins. Since we became interested in birds, Jimmy and I have searched for this owl over the salt marshes of coastal California, the sandy flats of Texas's Mustang Island, and clear-cut openings of southern Ontario. We have headed out at dusk with binoculars to a dozen places around the country, scouring a variety of flat landscapes in the hope of seeing the big bird with the buoyant, floppy flight of a giant moth. But we never found it.

One fall while Jeff was visiting, he and I walked our property in search of migrants. We began our hike in the garden, walked down through the woods, and then climbed the hill on the east side of the sanctuary. When we reached the end of the trail, we turned toward the sumac that runs alongside the woods on the south side of the property. From an opening in the sumac, a flash of gold and white burst from the ground and vanished over the top of the hill.

"That was a short-eared owl, Mom," Jeff said.

My birding instincts to speak softly and move slowly were overwhelmed by excitement. I danced around shouting, "I can't believe it! A short-eared owl right here on our property!"

Although it was a life bird, which is one seen for the first time, I couldn't count it. In my fervor, I hadn't really looked at the bird but had only caught a glimpse of it as it exploded from the field. I had seen none of its field marks.

Jeff came to the rescue. He saw where it had landed and led me slowly up the hill. Just over the crest, less than twenty yards away, was the owl. It had dropped back to the ground in front of the dense branches of a small downed tree. The leafy green background contrasted with the tawny earth tones of the owl's feathers, framing it perfectly.

Its large yellow eyes studied us intently from the pale center of a round, flat face. A pair of tiny feather tufts, the "ears" for which it is named, stood close together on top of its head. Nearly white feathers on the belly and breast were streaked with brown and buff, and its golden, feathery pantaloons grew all the way to its toes.

We watched the owl silently, savoring its elegant beauty for several minutes. Then we left it alone to roost in peace.

Short-eared owls have disappeared from many of their former nesting areas across our country and are declining in some places where they are still found. They are currently classified as endangered in several states, including Michigan. They are rare visitors to our area; there have been only three other recorded sightings of this species in Leelanau County. Habitat degradation is the likely cause of the short-eared owl's declining numbers.

As crazy as I am about Tom Graham's magnificent steam engine, it is reminder that too often human activities have destroyed habitat for those with whom we share this planet like the short-eared owl. It was, after all, engines like the Avery that made the first serious inroads into North America's vast prairies. This destruction was carried out by people who saw no end to the possibilities for exploiting the nation's land, water, and natural resources. Because we all have to eat and each of us needs a place to live, both agriculture and development will necessarily continue. But we are beginning to understand that farming, lumbering, and development should not destroy every vestige of the natural world. They do not have to. Farmers can leave hedgerows, loggers can cut selectively or use clearcuts in moderation, and developers can build around the most significant habitats.

19

THE ASTONISHING RUBY-THROAT

I sat down at my desk one afternoon in early September to write a note to the program director of an Audubon club that had asked me to present a slide program. I needed to confirm the schedule, but the program director's address and phone number had vanished into the pile of papers on my desk along with a number of other important items including two new books of stamps. I sifted through the stack without finding either the address or the stamps. It was hopeless. My desk had become quicksand. The harder I fought to keep it all straight, the lower anything essential sank.

I gave up on my search and turned away from my desk to see what was at the feeder on the other side of my window. A very young ruby-throated hummingbird hovered at the nectar feeder, probing its bill through the port and slipping its thread-thin tongue into the sugar water inside.

The bird appeared to be too young to be on its own. Fledgling birds are easily recognized by a plump appearance similar to the chubby look of young mammals. A fledgling also has a shorter tail and bill than an adult, but the most distinctive and easy-to-spot characteristic is the "gape." A bird's gape is the soft corner of the mouth around the hinge of the bill. In baby birds this area is enlarged, fleshy, and often brightly colored. The hummer at our feeder was very plump, its bill and tail were short, and its fleshy gape was that of a baby bird.

How it had found his way to our artificial nectar was a mystery. Its mother, which should still have been nearby supplying the young bird with tiny insects, was nowhere to be seen. For several hours the fledgling alternately took our nectar and then sat on top of the shepherd's crook that held the feeder. While there was an unlimited supply of sugar water for this little bird, it didn't appear to be old enough to capture insects. Only about half of a hummingbird's nutritional requirements are met by nectar; the rest comes from minute insects that provide needed protein.

At dawn the next morning the fat little hummer was still hanging around. Although it had been a chilly night, the bird looked in good condition when it took its place again on top of the shepherd's crook. That evening, as the sun faded, the young hummer zipped off its perch to snatch a flying insect. It stayed for two weeks, hogging the feeder outside the window. During that time, I watched the hummingbird develop much as I had the eastern kingbird we had cared for, and pondered the magnificent journey it was about to undertake. Soon it would begin the migration south. For the first few weeks of migration, this minuscule, high-energy, warm-blooded machine would feed its way down to the Gulf Coast. Frequent stops at feeders and nectar-bearing flowers along the way would allow it to build fat reserves that would add 40 percent to its body weight.

By October, the hummingbird would reach the coast of Louisiana or Texas where its feeding frenzy would continue. Then one afternoon, with a steady breeze drifting down from the north, this tiny bird would turn from its flowers and fly straight south over the open water of the Gulf of Mexico. When the sun rose the next morning, it would still be in the air, alone.

Hummingbirds, unlike shorebirds and some songbirds, are solitary migrants. There would be no reassuring voices of its own kind to encourage this Lilliputian youngster along as there are with other species.

Fueled by its extra fat, the hummingbird would finally reach its destination on Mexico's Yucatan Peninsula eighteen to twenty-four hours after lifting off from this country. Its non-stop flight of four hundred to five hundred miles would leave it in a state of total exhaustion, and by the time it landed, the hummingbird would have lost fully half its body weight. After resting, it would begin to feed again before moving as far south as Costa Rica to spend the winter. In March, the hummingbird would begin the entire process again in reverse, finding its way back to the precise place where it began life the year before.

An adult ruby-throated hummingbird not only will find its way back to the same territory every year of its life, it remembers the exact location of a feeder it previously frequented. If it returns to find that its feeder has not yet been put up, it will scold its benefactor for the oversight.

If our little bird were a female, her life would be even more complex and difficult than that of her mate. After a brief encounter with the male of her choice, a female ruby-throat is left alone to build her nest, incubate her eggs, feed her nestlings, and care for her fledglings without any aid from any quarter. She accomplishes all of these things while keeping up with her own extraordinary energy requirements. Every day this bird must find hundreds of very small insects in order to survive, and she visits up to three thousand flowers just to satisfy her own high-energy needs.

She fashions her miniature cuplike nest by stitching fine plant fibers and plant down together with spider's silk. As she works, she periodically perches inside the developing cup and presses her belly against the sides to shape the nest. She keeps the upper edge thin, curving it inward to keep the eggs and hatchlings from tumbling out. Once finished, she adds tiny bits of lichen to the outside for camouflage.

A female hummingbird finishes homebuilding in less than a week. Then she lays two eggs inside and incubates them for about two weeks. During that time she flies off briefly to feed as often as sixty times a day. For three to four weeks after her chicks hatch, her life is a nonstop effort to find food for herself and her hatchlings. All avian youngsters need large amounts of protein for development, so from the time her chicks emerge, our little mother hummer must catch an additional two thousand insects daily for each of her babies. By the time they leave the nest, they will be fatter than she is.

Incredibly, immediately after her offspring set out on their own, she may begin the entire process of rearing chicks again, although the second time she may use the same nest.

After watching the baby hummer at my window for a long time, I turned back to the pile of papers on my desk. The address I had misplaced lost its importance. Everything on my desk seemed trivial when compared to the astonishing life cycle of ruby-throated hummingbirds.

20

LIGHTHOUSE CREATURES

If I had to find work away from home, the job managing the gift shop for the lighthouse was as good as it could get. My shop was in the hundred-year-old Fog Signal Building that had originally housed a coal-fired boiler for the steam-powered fog signal at the tip of the Leelanau Peninsula. The building, located behind the lighthouse, was a quaint brick affair with a high tin ceiling inside and a cherry-red metal roof outside. It was filled with quality merchandise for lovers of lighthouses. Best of all, it was located a dozen steps from a wet woods that was home to a family of winter wrens. For the first three months I worked there, one of these tiny songsters serenaded me daily. What could be better than that?

A mix of rich habitats surrounded the building. Down a short path, a stony stretch of Lake Michigan shoreline offered nesting grounds for killdeer and spotted sandpipers. Giant maples in the yard supported a couple of Baltimore oriole families, an old bird apartment on a pole provided nest sites for tree swallows, and chimney swifts were attracted to the chimney on the lighthouse itself. Eastern kingbirds, American redstarts, great crested flycatchers, and other passerines sang just outside the doors and windows. It was the perfect place for a bird lover who had to punch a clock.

Moreover I enjoyed the job itself. Doug McCormick, a retired Coast Guard veteran, had lived in the lighthouse as a child and moved back into it after it was restored. He was the designated caretaker, but his role as archivist and ambassador was far more important. Every afternoon he came to visit me in the shop. People loved to hear him tell tales of life in the lighthouse. One man asked him if the old place was haunted.

"Oh, sure," Doug answered. Sometimes during a storm, he added, he thought he could hear his father making his way up the circular stairs to check on the light. No one will ever know whether or not Doug really believes the lighthouse is haunted; even if he didn't, he would never let an opportunity to tell a good story slip by.

I enjoyed Doug's stories as much as our visitors did. The tales of his childhood instilled a personal connection with the old light. Many times I was the last one out of the building at the end of the day. I·was aware, as I made my way through the rooms before locking up, that they looked very much as they did when Doug was a kid, and I wondered what it must be like to return to one's childhood home. Surely he must feel his family's presence when he walks through those rooms.

I also enjoyed having a chance to chat with the stream of people who loved the old light and appreciated the spectacular scenery around it. Many came in with binoculars hanging from their necks, and I always asked if they were birders. But for the first two months there wasn't one among them. They were water watchers all—looking at islands, passing ships, and the town of Charlevoix off in the distance across Grand Traverse Bay. In the middle of July, a woman with a relatively expensive pair of binoculars came through the door. Finally, I thought, a soul mate.

"Are you a birdwatcher?" I asked for the hundredth time.

"Oh yes!" she said enthusiastically. "I'm crazy about watching birds. I feed them in my yard in Chicago. My favorites are those brownish tan birds. You know, the ones you sometimes see in parking lots. I get lots of those."

I said I thought she was probably referring to house sparrows.

"Is that what they're called? Well, I just love them. I see them everywhere!"

The following week another visitor, with another pair of expensive binoculars hanging from his neck, said that he too was an avid birdwatcher.

"Whenever I see a bird I don't recognize, I grab my bird book and see if I can figure out what it is."

Success at last! Chasing down an unrecognized bird to determine its identity is Kenn Kaufman's definition of a birder. Kaufman is one of this country's best bird writers and a leading expert on the subject.

The man asked if I liked birds and I told him about our sanctuary.

"We manage it for migrating and nesting Neotropical passerines," I said.

He looked puzzled. Then he asked, "Would that be, like, pigeons?"

Well, partial success.

It wasn't until October that any real birders came into the shop. Three people from Illinois, upon learning of my interest, asked where they might go to find migrating raptors. It was almost closing time when they left, and on my way home I found them stopped alongside the road. I stopped and they asked if I could identify the hawk soaring overhead. It was a red-tailed hawk. They may have been beginners, but they were definitely real birders. Success at last.

Birds weren't the only wildlife around the Fog Signal Building. One morning a group of visiting school kids stumbled onto a newborn fawn. In order to lessen the stress on the doe, the lighthouse director rerouted the rest of the busload around the site.

A few days later, I heard a cry just outside the door. At first I thought it was a baby, then decided it sounded more like a puppy. It was a plaintive little sound, and when it persisted, I went to the open the door of my shop to investigate. There, looking up at me through enormous dark brown eyes, was the fawn. It was very small, heavily spotted, and still a wee bit wobbly. Its mother was nowhere to be seen, and it seemed to be begging.

Like too many of my own kind (and in spite of the fact that I know better), I made the assumption that the fawn had been abandoned, and I went back inside to call for help and then returned to the door to watch the young deer. Startled by my second appearance, it bolted into a nearby thicket. From there, it studied me through those beautiful eyes from its half-hiding place and continued its pitiful bleating. After a moment, the fawn rose from its spot, stood in place for another moment, and then took a cautious step back toward the open door. It took another step, poking its face out of the brush and, at that instant, its mother bounded in from the woods behind the building. I was only a few feet from the mother, and when she saw me, her tail shot straight up and fluffed like the fur of a spooked cat.

Not wanting to alarm her further, I backed slowly inside the building and watched through the window as she led her youngster into the woods. I didn't see them again until late fall when they wandered briefly out of the cedar swamp that had been home to the singing winter wren.

After the tourist season ended—taking with it most avian and human migrants—a woman wearing a diaphanous ankle-length skirt and a blouse with puffy sleeves came into the shop. She looked around briefly and then struck up a conversation, asking what I did when I wasn't selling pencils and post cards. She was a friendly, fiftyish woman with an easy smile. Something about her made me think of the flower children of the late sixties. Perhaps it was her hands that waved gracefully in the air as she talked, or maybe it was her style of dress and the way her long, graying hair flowed down her back from a wide barrette at the crown.

I told her that my husband and I manage our own bird sanctuary. She was very interested and wanted to know how we went about our work. I told her that the most important part of our work had been selecting a piece of property that offered a variety of good habitats, but did not tell her that I shoot starlings and try to drown their young. Then I asked what she did when she wasn't looking at lighthouses.

"I pursue God," she said dreamily.

Then, as quickly as the doe and fawn had slipped into the woods, she floated out the door and was gone, although in my mind's eye I could see her skipping across a flower-filled meadow with a giant butterfly net in hand.

21

ON WALDRON POND

"Every woman who loves birds needs a Jimmy or a Jack," said Nancy Waldron, referring to my husband and hers. "All you or I have to do is just mention that we have seen another pair of bluebirds on the property and our men will immediately build a new nest box and have it up before lunch."

Although we met the Waldrons at Goose Island State Park in Texas, they are from Burt Lake, Michigan, which is about two hours from our home. When we met them at Goose Island, they were camped on the shell reef there, as we were, while escaping the harsh winter back home. Like us, Jack and Nancy Waldron are birders concerned over vanishing habitat for the feathered creatures they love. They had both the means and the will to do something about it. The year before we bought our property, they closed on 158 acres of land east of Petoskey, Michigan. Then they created a permanent sanctuary by placing the land under a conservation easement.

Conservation easements are vehicles by which property owners can limit the uses of their land or prevent development of it in perpetuity while retaining ownership of that land. These easements are legally binding agreements entered into with either nonprofit land trusts, conservancies, or appropriate government agencies. The conservancy or land trust accepts full responsibility for enforcing the terms of the document. The landowner retains complete ownership. Because the Waldrons wanted to protect their land for future generations to enjoy, they entered such an agreement with a suitable local organization.

Nancy knew the property very well long before she and Jack ever entertained the idea of buying it. She had birded it for years, and it had always been a special place for her. They named their land "The Fen," after the large wetland in its center, but they call the pond tucked into the woods near the entrance "Waldron Pond."

Although we see the Waldrons most often during the winter in Arizona or Texas where we always get together for birding, we have made the two-hour drive from our place to theirs several times. The first time was the summer after we met them.

Waldron Pond is a quiet place, much like Thoreau's own Walden was more than 150 years ago when he sought to escape the "hurry and waste" of the outside world. Like Thoreau, the Waldrons often settle into a simple life on their refuge. Although they own an elegant home on the shores of Burt Lake, they prefer to spend much of their summer on their private sanctuary. A retired builder, Jack is a tall man with a warm smile and a passion for little birds. Spring is his favorite season when migration brings at least fifteen warbler species for him to watch as they feed their way across his property.

His energetic wife becomes more animated during the nesting season, especially when sandhill cranes settle down to nest on an island in the fen. When we visited them a few years ago, Nancy was sorry to report that a raccoon had taken one of the parent cranes.

"I don't think we'll have any crane chicks this year," she said sadly.

A few weeks later she called with exciting news. Unknown to her, the surviving crane had apparently found another mate— there was a leggy yellow hatchling on the island in the middle of the fen.

"I just found it this morning!" she said. "And I couldn't wait to tell someone who would be as thrilled as I am! The only problem is that I'm not sure it has enough time to develop before its parents leave, so I told Jack that if the youngster isn't ready to go when they are, we're just going to take it south with us!"

She might have done just that. If Jack is a songbird guy, Nancy is a crane freak. Every fall when they leave Michigan, they head straight for Bosque del Apache in New Mexico, winter home of tens of thousands of sandhills and site of an annual crane festival.

Before the middle of the 1800s, sandhill cranes nested in nearly every part of Michigan. But uncontrolled hunting and loss of wetland habitat decimated the population. The Migratory Bird Treaty Act of 1918 protected cranes from hunting, but habitat destruction led to further declines. In 1944 only twenty-seven pairs remained in Michigan's Lower Peninsula. State and federal wetland protection measures enabled the population of these stately birds to recover, and by the time the Waldrons bought their land, there were more than six hundred nesting pairs in the Lower Peninsula alone. For several years in a row, one pair chose the fen as its nesting place.

Waldron Pond includes a variety of habitats. Extensive fallow fields provide nest sites for bobolinks and upland sandpipers and the fen itself has provided nesting for breeding American bitterns. An old stand of pines is home to woodpeckers and great horned owls.

When we made our first visit to Waldron Pond, I was most interested in seeing the bittern, which Jimmy and I had seen only once before. We arrived just after noon on a raw spring day and followed our hosts along the trail to an observation platform Jack had built at the edge of the fen. Nancy played a tape of the bittern's call and told us where to watch for the bird. Moments later, a creature that looked like a leggy, brown-streaked version of Al Capp's schmoo waddled out from behind a clump of vegetation. Its round belly rested on long legs and supported a thick neck and head. Nancy played the tape again and the bittern increased its gait, issuing back the call that gave it the nickname "slough pump" or "thunder pumper"—a sound that has been variously described as *Oon-ka-chonk*, *Pump-per-link*, or *Oon-ka-lunk*.

I don't envy any man or woman's wealth or status. But I confess a bit of jealousy for the Waldron's fen with its nesting bitterns and their much larger meadow where upland sandpipers nest. My greatest hope is that someday we can buy more land for our sanctuary and thereby increase both its effectiveness and the number of species it serves.

22

In Search of the Great Kiskadee

In August I got a telephone call from Nancy.

"Is Jimmy packing up to leave for the Southwest?" she asked.

"It's only August, Nancy. Too early to think about our own migration."

"Tell that to the snow goose in our wetland. It came in last night, but it shouldn't have arrived until October. Do you suppose it knows something we don't?"

If the snow goose knew something the rest of us didn't, it kept it to itself. And it didn't leave until the normal migration was underway.

A few days after Nancy called about her early goose, I agreed to write a piece about the great kiskadee for *Texas Parks & Wildlife* magazine. The deadline was December 20, which would allow plenty of time for me to do the research during the first part of our annual winter birding trek. But family circumstances forced a change in plans; Jimmy was not able to leave in time for me to meet my deadline. My sister Chris accepted an invitation to travel with me to south Texas to look for kiskadees.

The purpose of our trip was two-fold: I wanted to observe kiskadees to get a better feel for their behavior, and I wanted to get good photographs of the bird to accompany my article. Though they are flycatchers, great kiskadees sometimes dive for small fish. My greatest hope was to snap a shot of a kiskadee snagging a fish from a stream—that would add the finishing touch to the article.

Belonging to a family of birds known as tyrant flycatchers (so named because its members are highly aggressive, especially during the breeding season), the great kiskadee is a big, beautiful flycatcher with bright lemon breast, rufous-red wings and tail, and bold black-and-white lateral head stripes. This colorful bird ranges from central Mexico down through Argentina and spills over into our country only in southeastern Texas, particularly in the lower Rio Grande Valley.

The American Birding Association puts out a series of books under the collective heading *Lane/ABA Birdfinding Guide*, which birders refer to simply as *Lane Guides*; they are very helpful when searching for new species in unfamiliar areas. According to the *Lane Guide* for the Rio Grande Valley, the great kiskadee is a "common permanent resident of woodlands near water from Laredo to the Gulf." It is "easy to find at Santa Ana National Wildlife Refuge and Bentsen-Rio Grande Valley State Park." The *Lane Guide* for the Texas coast also lists the bird in Kingsville.

We took along both guides. Before we left, I e-mailed Father Tom Pincelli, the best-known birder in the valley, to ask where we would be most apt to find the bird. The good padre responded that we would have no problem finding kiskadees in towns, in parks, and all along the river. They are everywhere, he said.

When Chris and I left for Texas, I had high hopes of finding and photographing the great kiskadee. It seemed an easy task. I was mistaken.

Our first stop was Kingsville. During our winters in Rockport, Jimmy and I regularly made day-trips with birding friends to Kingsville, where we never failed to see at least one kiskadee—nearly always along Santa Gertrudis Creek. Chris and I planned to look there first. We arrived in town before lunch, had a quick bite, and went straight to the creek. When we failed to find the bird, we went to Dick Kleberg Park. A great egret stalked fish from the edge of the spillway, and a belted kingfisher issued his trademark rattlelike call from a tree on the opposite bank. Best of all, a vermilion flycatcher, the smallest and most brilliant North American flycatcher, sallied out from a nearby branch to snag an insect. Chrissy was captivated by the tiny red bird, which Mexicans call *la brasita de fuego*, which translates to "little coal of fire." But there were no kiskadees in Dick Kleberg Park that day.

We went next to the cemetery. Cemeteries often provide productive birding, and the Chamberlain Cemetery in Kingsville is especially good. The large old trees, according to the *Lane Guide*, host numerous nesting birds including brown-crested flycatchers, green jays, and great kiskadees. The trees in the cemetery and the brushy edges surrounding it were alive with birds, but the kiskadee was not among them.

The following day we retraced our route, spending time again at the park, the creek, and the cemetery. Before we left town we also explored the campus of Texas A & I University, where, according to the guidebook, one should look for great kiskadees "at all seasons." But there were no kiskadees at either the park, the creek, the cemetery, or the campus that November day. Reluctantly, we gave up on Kingsville and left for the valley.

The Lower Rio Grande Valley is not a valley at all but a broad, flat riparian zone that drains into the Rio Grande. It was once a floodplain covered with dense thickets and subtropical vegetation. Today, however, upstream dams have dramatically reduced the river's flow, and downstream levees harness what little water remains. Farms, citrus groves, and cities have replaced most of the natural habitat, but islands of original thickets and forests remain in places like Santa Ana National Wildlife

Refuge, Bentsen-Rio Grande Valley State Park, and the Audubon Society's Sabal Palm Grove Sanctuary. We began our search at the refuge, where Jimmy and I had had our first look at a great kiskadee years earlier.

The day after we arrived, Chris and I arose at dawn, had a quick breakfast, and left the motel immediately. We pulled into the refuge parking lot before the visitor center opened. A volunteer was about to lead several people on a bird walk along the trail to Willow Lake. We joined the group and said that we were looking for kiskadees and particularly hoped to find them fishing. One of the women said that we'd just missed a small flock in the parking lot. She added that they may have been pushed back into the refuge by a busload of birders from the Harlingen Bird Festival, which was taking place that weekend.

"That's okay," our guide said. "We'll see them on this walk. They're always down by the lake."

The place was full of hungry mosquitoes that attacked Chrissy en masse and raised great red welts all over her face and arms. Our guide had Benadryl tablets in his pack and gave her one. He also had some mosquito repellent, which she used to minor benefit.

We reached the photo blind at Willow Lake and stopped to look for our bird, aided by the others in our little group. But there were no kiskadees. We stayed with the birders until they left the wide trail and turned off onto a narrow path through the dense brush. Chris was nervous about following, fearing the snakes she was certain lurked in the vegetation crowding the path. My fear of snakes has kept me from many a bird walk, but I could have managed the path at the refuge. I didn't know until then that Chris is even worse than I am—but I should have. In our first motel after leaving home, she had stuffed newspapers in the crack under the door because she feared a nighttime visitor. I tried to tell her that we were unlikely to find a snake on a cold night in the heart of Muskogee, but she would have none of it. The paper went under the door before she climbed into bed.

As the group disappeared into the brush, she confessed that she wasn't even comfortable with the wide concrete walk we were on. We returned to the parking lot, and I made some quick mental changes to the plans I'd worked up for finding this bird. If my kid sister was good enough to accompany me on this venture, I was only too happy to work out a strategy she would be entirely comfortable with.

Chris had developed an interest in lighthouses, and there is a historic light at Port Isabel along the Intracoastal Waterway about an hour from Santa Ana. We had planned to visit it while we were in the valley, so I suggested we put irritating insects and reptile fears aside and take a short break from our birding. We would drive over to the coast, check out the lighthouse, find a place for lunch, and then go up to Laguna Atascosa National Wildlife Refuge, which also hosts kiskadees.

But when we got to Port Isabel, we found the lighthouse girdled by scaffolding and enshrouded at the top with a heavy fabric. It was closed for restoration, a deep disappointment for Chris. We walked around the perimeter of the light and tried to imagine it without all the paraphernalia hanging from it. Then we went inside the visitor's center and asked the volunteer at the desk for a recommendation for lunch.

"The place across the street is wonderful," she said. "The seafood is great and the bread is to kill for."

We took her suggestion. But the food was terrible. On our way back to the car, we agreed that our effort to find a bird reputed to be virtually everywhere was failing miserably. We weren't even able to get a diversionary side trip or a midday meal right. With sagging spirits, we headed north to Laguna Atascosa, fully expecting to fail again.

But as we turned from the highway into the visitor's center, a kiskadee flew across the road in front of us. Then there was another and another. They worked their way across the shrubby cover between the parking lot and the road, stopping at a bush not far from the car to feast on berries. We watched the birds for the rest of the afternoon as they foraged in a wide circle around the visitor's center and parking lot, but they were an active lot and provided no opportunities for photos.

First thing the next morning we were back at Santa Ana. The birding guide, who knew we were researching an article about the bird, told us we had missed a fishing kiskadee the day before.

"Almost as soon as you left us on the trail," he said, "a kiskadee dove down from a branch to snag a minnow from a little stream."

I asked him if he knew of any old nests we might photograph. He didn't, but suggested that we speak with Dave Blankinship, a wildlife biologist at Santa Ana and a lifelong birder. He was certain that Dave would be able to direct us to a nest.

We left Santa Ana and drove to Bentsen-Rio Grande Valley State Park, following Military Road rather than the highway. There was a place along an irrigation ditch just outside the park where Jimmy and I had always found all three kingfishers that occur in the valley—belted, ringed, and green. Belted kingfishers range widely across North America, but both the ringed and green—like the kiskadee—are tropical birds that spill across the Rio Grande. Sadly, when we reached the ditch, we found that every shrub and tree had been cut away from the banks, leaving no place for the kingfishers to perch and hunt for food.

At Bentsen, a woman told Chris that we should have been at her campsite earlier in the day. There, she said, she watched kiskadees at her feeder.

"There were hundreds of them," the woman had said. "They were all over the place."

"What do you think?" Chris asked me later.

"I think it's not bloody likely," I said. "I don't think they are that social."

We asked Dave Blankinship that question when we met with him the next day. Blankinship, a friendly man with an easy smile, welcomed us into his small office in the interior of the refuge headquarters at the appointed hour.

"Hundreds of kiskadees in a flock?" he asked, repeating our question. "No. At this time of year, you might see a family grouping of five or six individuals, but not hundreds."

Blankinship has a passion for great kiskadees that goes back more than forty years. He recalled the first time he ever saw one. It was in the midfifties.

"I was a field assistant for the Texas Game, Fish and Oyster Commission," he said. "I was involved in a population study of white-winged doves in the Lower Rio Grande Valley. It was my job to observe nests in a number of specific sites in order to document predation and production of the doves. One afternoon, while I was working along a drainage ditch north of McAllen, I saw something I have never forgotten. A bird that I didn't recognize was foraging for fish over the ditch. I was astonished by this bird. I was struck by its size and by its bold black-and-white head. I knew most of the avian species of the valley at the time, and I knew all of the kingfishers in the area, but I'd never seen anything like this bird before."

The man who would later become a wildlife biologist was in his teens at the time, and he wanted very much to know what kind of bird he had seen, so he made a drawing of it and took it to his boss, W.H. Kiel, Jr., a field biologist for the commission. Kiel immediately recognized the bird as a derby flycatcher. The name was later changed to kiskadee flycatcher, which then became great kiskadee.

Blankinship marveled at how well kiskadees have fared in the Rio Grande Valley despite an active agricultural sector and a rapidly growing human population.

"This was a rare bird when I first saw it," he said. "Now I would call it abundant. It is a frequent visitor to my backyard birdbath. I've seen as many as five individuals at a time in my yard."

The interview was helpful for my article, but it didn't help with photographs—even of an old nest. The accommodating wildlife biologist didn't know where we might find one.

In spite of coming away without any usable photos, the trip was wonderful. I not only learned a great deal about the kiskadee, I was able to introduce my kid sister to the joys of birding with species she might otherwise never see.

23

A TASTY THANKSGIVING DINNER

Sometime in September I talked to a local bird hunter who was working with the Leelanau Conservancy to develop guidelines for a significant tract of land the Conservancy had obtained. His name was Paul, and he liked to "fill his freezer with wood-cock and grouse." He also raised pheasants, as do several other hunters in our area.

I called Paul to invite him to walk our property with me because I had been told by a mutual acquaintance that he be-lieved the decline in the birds he wanted to hunt was the result of fewer stands of young aspen. I'm by no means an expert in either habitat or bird populations, but I do know that both grouse and woodcock are thriving on our property where there are no young stands of aspen. I thought if we did some exploring, we might both learn something.

When Paul answered the telephone, I introduced myself. He knew of our sanctuary and its location. He and I weren't able to settle on a date, but he was surprised to learn that we had both of the species he is so interested in. During our conversation, he said that he trains his dogs on a nearby parcel and asked if he could hunt birds here. I told him he couldn't. He took my refusal in good humor and we hung up.

A week later, seven young pheasants showed up and took to picking around in our garden. I immediately e-mailed Jeff a message entitled "New Yard Bird."

> Dear Jeff,
>
> Got a new bird hanging around; someone must have released a flock of young pheasants either on or near our land. They have now adopted the place as home. I won't be too happy about the possibility of having them nest here, however...I'm sure they displace native species. If they survive the winter, we'll just have to solve the problem with a few good pheasant dinners!
>
> Love,
> Mom

His immediate response:

> Hi Ma,
>
> About the pheasants: Eat 'em! Don't wait to see if they nest, just plug 'em 'n cook 'em!
>
> Chow,
> JW

Unlike ruffed grouse and woodcock, which are native to northern Michigan and veritable symbols of the north woods, ring-necked pheasants are among the handful of game birds brought to North America in the late nineteenth century for the purpose of hunting. This handsome species established significant breeding populations in many parts of the United States and Canada, particularly in Great Plains states. Southern Michigan has had some huntable, year-round populations of pheasants. But pheasants never established themselves in the northern parts of Michigan where we live because they can't survive the winters. And because they are exotics, and exotics tend to displace native species, they aren't welcome on our property.

But as game birds, pheasants are protected out of season throughout the state. Happily, pheasant season in Michigan would begin before I left for Texas. Neither Jimmy nor I are hunters, but our friend Marlin Bussey is. When we first saw the birds, we made a deal with Marn; if he got the pheasants, we would share them for Thanksgiving dinner. Immediately after the deal was made, the birds vanished.

As soon as the pheasant season opened, Marn brought his shotgun and hiked the property looking for them. When I returned from a trip to town, Marn was back from his hunt and having coffee with Jimmy. I asked if he had found the pheasants.

"No," he said. "But I could have shot three grouse."

"Sorry, Marn," I said. "You can't shoot the grouse. You can have all the pheasants you can fix your sight on, but I love seeing our grouse and I'd like to keep them around."

We hadn't seen the pheasants for weeks before Marn came that day, but several days later, three of them showed up under the feeder. I called Marn.

"Bring your gun," I said.

He arrived within minutes and then Blam! Blam!...we had our meal.

I pulled a tail feather from one bird and sent it to Jeff and Becky, who were coming for the holiday, along with a note saying: "Guess who's coming for dinner?"

24

CONVERSION TO CONSERVATIONIST

Jimmy has known Pat and Marlin Bussey virtually all of his life. Jimmy and Marn were in the same class at school, and they both began their working careers for Dow Chemical Company in Midland, Michigan, at roughly the same time. Marn stayed with the company, but all it took for Jimmy to leave his home state was one winter trip to southern California. With that, he quit his job and moved to San Diego, where I met him a few years later.

Along the way, Marn was transferred to Ohio. We had dinner with the Busseys one evening at their Ohio home the year we began our three-year continental tour. It was October and hunting season was just around the corner. Marn is a lifelong hunter and that night over dinner he talked a great deal about hunting. I decided immediately that I definitely did not like this man. He was a killer of wild things.

At the time I was something of an animal rights advocate.

While meat was part of my diet, I would never dream of killing a wild animal for any reason. In my mind, to do so was just plain wrong. When my brother and his wife gave me a felt hat for Christmas the year after we visited the Busseys, I took it back and exchanged it for a straw one. My brother tried to tell me that beavers—from whose pelts felt is made—had to be controlled in some places because their numbers were so high they caused problems. I would have none of it.

On camping trips, I fed peanuts to squirrels and popcorn to raccoons. Any spider in the house was trapped under a drinking glass and hauled outside. One evening when I was on my way home from work in southern California, a hefty rattlesnake crawled across my path, and I carefully steered around it, even though the snake was only a few hundred yards away from our front door and I am absolutely terrified of snakes...especially poisonous ones.

I still trap spiders and carry them outdoors, and I would still avoid running over the rattler, even though I continue to be terrified by snakes. But I no longer feed squirrels and raccoons—and I've changed my mind about felt hats. I've also changed my mind about Marlin Bussey.

Marn retired, and he and Pat moved back to Leelanau County the same year that Jimmy and I bought our first bed-and-breakfast here. We spent a lot of time with the Busseys, and I came to know Marn for the kind-hearted and gentle man he is. No one has been better to us than these two generous, caring people. Today I think of them as our closest friends, and I love Marn like a brother.

If it was Dave Brigham who taught me the benefit to songbirds of reducing the squirrel population, it was Marn who taught me how to follow Dave's example. Jimmy and I spent seven weeks living with the Busseys when we were building the house we now live in. We stayed in the large walkout basement that amounts to a private apartment without a kitchen; it has three bedrooms, a bathroom, and a large family room. I was working at my typewriter late one afternoon, and Marn came down the stairs with his pellet gun and stood at the door of the family room.

"Okay," he said. "It's your turn."

The red squirrel population on their property had exploded that year, as it had the year before at our place when we lived next to Dave. Marn had been working to bring the rodents under control with his pellet gun. We had talked over dinner about how we were going to manage our sanctuary, and he knew that one thing I was determined to do was to protect our songbirds from nest depredation.

When he appeared at the door of the family room that day and told me it was my turn, I knew exactly what he meant. But there was a problem; with the exception of flies, mosquitoes, and tomato worms, I had never killed a living thing in my life. Inside my chest beat the heart of a woman who still carried spiders outdoors in a drinking glass.

The memory of the beautiful little redstart, which had failed at both attempts to nest in a tree behind our home, nudged me from my chair, and I joined our friend with a shaking hand. Adrenaline filled my bloodstream and I felt faint as I aimed his gun. My heart raced, a knot formed in my gut, and my knees turned to jelly. Determined to do what was needed, I steadied my hand and fired.

"Good girl," Marn said when the pellet found its mark.

I returned to my chair and tried to calm my quivering frame.

If our friend hadn't provided that first lesson, I don't know if I would ever have been able to bring myself to shoot a squirrel. As it is, even though I make jokes about doing it, my knees still turn to butter every time I capture a squirrel in the crosshairs of my gun. For Marn, it wasn't quite so hard. He has always understood the role of hunting and trapping in maintaining a balance in the natural world. Until Jimmy and I became more intimately involved with that world, I did not.

While what I don't know greatly exceeds what I do know, I am now aware that nature is both terrible and wonderful. Consider the cheetah pulling down a Thompson's gazelle on the African savannah. This same animal, which inflicts violent death on a delicate and beautiful antelope, also tenderly cares for her cubs. Her killing not only provides for her and her offspring, it keeps the antelope population in check.

In a healthy ecosystem, Mother Nature maintains an exquisite balance between predator and prey. An increase in prey triggers a rise in the numbers of predators. Increased predators then reduce the population of prey, which in turn precipitates a drop in predators. If the cheetah did not kill the gazelle, she and her cubs would quickly die. In the long run, so would the gazelle. Without the controlling effect of the cheetah, antelope numbers would soon explode and their appetites would eventually outstrip their habitat. Then, barring the appearance of another predator or disease, they would starve in massive numbers. Before they starved, however, they would destroy critical habitat—not just for themselves but for other creatures as well.

In many places in the eastern part of our own country, excessive numbers of white-tailed deer devour vegetation until nothing is left for other animals with whom they share the forests. It is easy to spot the overpopulated areas by the browse line deer create when they strip every leaf from ground level up to about four to five feet.

In the 1980s, a U. S. Forest Service biologist began a study on the effect of this kind of overbrowse on nesting birds in Pennsylvania forest plots. The biologist fenced several plots, put small deer herds inside, and then tracked bird populations on each plot for ten years. He documented the fact that higher deer numbers result in fewer individual birds in each plot. He also noted that there were fewer numbers of overall species. Some, like indigo buntings, least flycatchers, and cerulean warblers, disappeared altogether.

The disappearance of cerulean warblers in the study is a bit of a mystery, and it indicates that the number of nesting birds lost to overbrowse is not limited to those whose nests fall below the browse line. Cerulean warblers are canopy creatures that build their nests from fifteen to ninety feet off the forest floor—high above the browse line.

When I asked Jeff if he knew why ceruleans disappeared from overbrowsed areas, he said that he did not. He added that this apparent phenomenon is an example of how many unanswered questions remain about the requirements of nesting songbirds. He suggested that the disappearance of the warblers

might have resulted from the fact that the insects on which they depend require understory vegetation for survival, and when the vegetation is stripped, the insects vanish and the birds disappear.

The Pennsylvania biologist limited his study to forest tracts. If he had included other types of habitat like thickets and wetlands, the numbers of songbird species lost would have been much higher. One evening when Tom Ford was visiting, we discussed the problem of overbrowse in our county and counted the numbers of avian species that nest beneath the browse line. There were more than forty for our county alone. And for those forty species, the damage done by overbrowse is no less devastating than it would be if a bulldozer came in and pushed out every tree, shrub, and blade of grass.

We have deer on our property, but their numbers are limited. If they ever reach the point where they threaten the habitat, I will call on our hunter friend to take one or two for his table.

25

SUNDAY-MORNING FISHERMAN

My sister Judy called from Tucson on Thanksgiving with a holiday greeting. During our conversation, she asked what she should do about a Cooper's hawk that had taken up residence in her yard. I said that the standard procedure was to stop feeding, and she replied that they had already done that, but the hawk stayed anyway.

Before she hung up she added, "By the way, our goldfish are disappearing from the pond again."

"Probably the same culprit as before," I said.

"Probably is, although we haven't seen him."

Judy bought her home in 1973 at what was then the edge of Tucson. It was located on a hillside in a neighborhood surrounded by desert vegetation. The front looks across what was once cactus and mesquite to the pine-topped peaks of the Catalina Mountains. It was a spectacular view. It still is, in spite of the fact that most of the desert vegetation has been removed for construction. Her backyard, however, was another story. There caliche soil scraped clean of every leaf or twig reflected the scorched-earth policy of too many builders, which is to eliminate every living thing in order to facilitate work on the project.

I fell in love with her home the first time I saw it, although my sometime gardener hands itched to dig holes in the dirt behind her house and drop desert plants into them. She did plant a drought-tolerant pine tree and a couple of Mexican fan palms. With that she was satisfied, and I ignored my impulse to make suggestions or to grab a pick and shovel.

Over the years, housing developments spouted up around her. In time native plants also poked up in the little caliche patch. My sister and her husband do not have a large yard, but as volunteer palo verde trees and mesquite bushes matured (along with her pine and palm trees), it became a natural island in an expanding sea of homes. A variety of birds began to call. Some moved in to stay. Cactus wrens—my favorite desert birds—set up housekeeping in the recesses of dead fronds hanging around the palm tree's trunk. Gambel's quail scratched in grassy clumps in search of seeds, and a gila woodpecker took to drumming on a rooftop vent pipe. As more species moved in, Judy became increasingly interested in them. She put out food, which brought birds in for closer observation.

Judy and her husband added a water feature to their bi-level backyard. It's a large and beautiful affair, with a twelve-by-eight-foot lower pond and a smaller upper pool. Water is circulated from the lower pond to the upper pool, and from there it cascades over two side-by-side rocky falls back into the lower pond.

The birds in her yard went crazy over this addition, and it attracted still more avian species. Judy's favorite pastime became watching resident Anna's hummingbirds drop in for a shower in the mist around one of the waterfalls.

There were some surprises. A hermit thrush spent time there one winter, and a lazuli bunting took advantage of the waterfall shower during migration that same year. Flocks of cedar waxwings and Lawrence's goldfinches dropped in for a

drink and a bath. But the biggest surprise came one spring
while we camped next to her home in our motor home. Not
long after we arrived, Judy expressed puzzlement at a gradual
decline in the goldfish she had planted in the pond.

"I'm sure they're breeding," she said. "There are lots of
little guys, but I can't figure out what's happening to the big
ones."

She asked Jimmy and me whether we had any idea what
might be taking her fish. Her yard is fenced, which keeps out
raccoons and neighborhood cats that might snare them. An
avian culprit seemed likely, but the only birds in that part of
the world that take fish are herons, egrets, and kingfishers. We
couldn't imagine any of these species coming into her urban
yard without someone seeing it. The mystery, it seemed, would
go unsolved.

But one Sunday morning as I watched the colorful parade
of desert species visit the feeding station we had set up outside

our motor home, a great blue heron flew in from the west. It perched on top of a utility pole along a wide, overgrown easement behind Judy's backyard and, after a brief survey of the scene, made a short hop to the top of her roof. From there it eyed the pond for long minutes, then cautiously dropped into the yard.

I left the rig quietly, went into her house, and told her the mystery of her lost fish was solved—and said that the beautiful, long-legged fisherman was still at his work. She ran to grab her camera to snap a shot of the heron. Unfortunately something spooked it before she got back to the window.

When I left the house to go back to the motor home, the big bird flew right over my head in the direction of a local fishing lake. It had been sitting on her roof the entire time she and I were talking about it just a few feet below.

When goldfish began disappearing again before her Thanksgiving call, she wasn't sure they were going to another (or the same) heron. But a couple of months later, she had surgery, and several Sunday mornings in a row she missed church while in recovery. The first Sunday she looked out of her bedroom window and saw the great bird at the edge of her pond. It was there again on Wednesday, when she and her husband typically attended a midweek church service, and again the following Sunday.

"This bird has figured out that both of us are always gone on Wednesday evening and Sunday morning," she said. "And that's when it comes to fish."

When she told her husband about the heron's return, he wanted to know what they were going to do about their fish.

"Nothing," she said.

"But I like goldfish," he protested.

"So does the heron."

26

WINTER TRACKS

There are many other creatures on our sanctuary besides birds. We've seen fox on the hillside and otter in the creek. A southern bog lemming scooted along the edge of the wetland one afternoon; muskrats wend their way around cattails snipping off marsh marigold blossoms; and for years deer have followed a narrow track that we eventually widened into Friendship Trail. There have also been skunks, shrews, opossums, voles, chipmunks, woodchuck, weasels, and raccoons. Every spring a porcupine tries to eat its way into our house, and we once saw a bobcat loping across the yard outside our kitchen window. Coyotes have been regular visitors, and when we first moved here, cottontails came out of our thickets and brushpiles nightly.

Then the coyote population exploded. When it did, the fox disappeared and the rabbits vanished except on rare occasions.

During warm months, almost anything could travel across

this land without our knowledge unless it was close to the house. But a snowstorm before we left for our annual trip to the Southwest left no secrets about which animals visited or where they went. Everything left tracks. Checking tracks in the snow on our land was a new experience; we've always been out of the state before the first snowfall. The first thing we noticed were deer trails crisscrossing the hillside across from the house. That was not surprising—we often watch deer browsing on that hillside from the comfort of our living room. But we were surprised when rabbit tracks appeared, and before long the yard became a patchwork quilt of the distinctive tracks of cottontails—two large back prints with two smaller prints in front. Obviously a few rabbits were holding their own against the coyotes, or nature's balance was beginning to swing again in favor of the bunnies.

Blue jays and mourning doves left little bird-feet impressions in the sheltered area under the wide eaves of the house. And five ruffed grouse left a trail when they walked along the edge of the yard on their way to the wild grapes intertwining pin cherry branches. Then I noticed little depressions that looked as though they had been made by someone gently dropping an apricot onto the snow and then carefully pulling it back out. Nothing connected the depressions—no tracks from bird or animal that might offer a clue as to what was creating the hollow shape. But as I studied the marks in the snow, a chickadee plucked a seed it had stored under a piece of bark, tapped it open with its bill, and then belly flopped straight down from the branch it was sitting on to pick up the leavings. When the chickadee flew away it left a perfect apricot-shaped depression in the snow. Mystery solved.

The next day mourning dove feathers littered the snow under the pin cherries. A Cooper's hawk had settled in to feed on our birds. We were faced with a dilemma: Should we take our feeders down or leave them up? Bird feeders concentrate songbirds, and that concentration attracts aerial predators like sharp-shinned and Cooper's hawks. While accipiters—sharpies, Cooper's, and goshawks—are a necessary part of the balance, feeders concentrate birds in artificially high numbers,

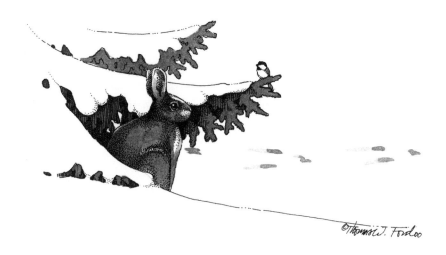

making a hawk's job easier and putting songbirds at an unnaturally high risk.

There is some evidence in New England that increasing numbers of accipiters no longer migrate, preferring instead hang around feeders where they find plenty to sustain them through the cold months. According to an article in the *New York Times*, the president of the Connecticut Ornithological Society said that virtually all the birds visiting his feeder one winter were taken by a sharp-shinned hawk. This man reported losing twenty to twenty-five songbirds over the course of that winter.

The protocol when an accipiter begins lurking around one's feeder is to stop feeding for a couple of weeks, which forces feeder visitors to disperse. The accipiters are then made to work for a living by having to hunt over a wider area. Preliminary research suggests that birds do not depend entirely on human offerings, and, in fact, when Jimmy and I leave for the winter, we make no special provisions for the birds that are permanent residents on our sanctuary. The rich habitat on our land provides for the birds that live here as well as those that visit. With the arrival of the Copper's hawk on our property, we decided to take the feeders down for the year.

The year after we bought our property, we worked up a

habitat development plan with the help of a wildlife biologist and a forester. The plan provided a blueprint for us to follow in order to manage alterations we wanted to make. The greatest change would be around the periphery of our western forty acres where we wanted a relatively narrow shrubby-woodsy buffer between the county roads bordering our property and our upland meadows.

Creating this ribbon of plantings, the interior edge of which would meander in a natural way, was a daunting affair for two people with limited time and resources. The perimeter is, after all, a full three-quarters of a mile long. It would take many thousands of seedlings purchased from the local soil conservation office as well as hundreds of transplants from areas we want to keep open. We began planting seedlings along the perimeter the year we bought the land.

Two years later, we bought, among other things, a dozen river birch seedlings, and we planted them in a damp corner of the property. Within three years, all but two of the original twelve trees were gone. Other seedlings we had planted had failed also, but none suffered the high attrition rate of the little river birches. We couldn't figure out what happened to the rest of our trees until the day I watched the chickadee flop into the snow for scraps.

Something speeding across our field, accompanied by the nerve-shattering sound of a two-cycle engine, caught my eye. It was a snowmobile. Another snowmobile raced along behind it. We soon learned that neighbors drove them. One of the neighbors is the volunteer fireman who was the first on our property when the call went out about our burning barn. Another lives across the road from us. These are people who are ordinarily kind and considerate—people we like and respect. But once these nice, ordinarily law-abiding citizens mount the backs of their motorized beasts, they become crazed criminals who drive roughshod over anything and everything. Some of them are radical about property rights; if we had the temerity to hunt— or even birdwatch—on their property without permission, they would be less than kind about our incursion. When the first track cut across the top of one of the two remaining river birch saplings that winter, I suggested to one of the culprits through my fury that I was tempted to string piano wire up around the perimeter of our land. His response? "If you put any barricade up that causes an injury to one of us, you will be liable—even though we are trespassing."

Several years earlier, the Michigan United Conservation Clubs, a state conservation organization, tried to pass legislation that would forbid the use of ATVs on private property even if it wasn't posted. The bill would also have mandated license numbers that are large enough for property owners like us to see from a distance. The powerful snowmobile lobby was able to scratch the provision on license numbers. They allowed the first part to pass, perhaps because they knew that without a way to identify the rider, there was no way to enforce it.

The following summer we moved some of our larger trees to the perimeter and erected "No Trespassing" signs. In the meantime, the only way we will be able to protect the plantings around the outside edge of our land will be to establish a trail for these snowmobilers, even though we do not want them on our property. If we don't, they will just go wherever they like. They may do so anyway.

Before we returned from our western trek, the snow melted and took the snowmobiles with it. But they didn't leave until they broke down more of the little trees we had planted at the edge. Then, during the first warm day after we were back, a four-wheeler rolled through an orchard across the road from us. When he got to the end of the orchard, the driver turned and cut across the corner of our land where our two remaining river birches struggled to survive against mechanical mayhem.

We don't complain about off-roaders just to be cranky property owners; we welcome visitors who want to see our birds and learn something about how we manage our sanctuary. But people who wander willy-nilly through the woods and across meadows during the breeding season put ground-nesting birds at risk, and snowmobiles and ATVs at any time of year crush carefully created habitat. If we could afford it, we would stretch fencing around the perimeter. Since we can't, we will just hope that we can protect what we have and direct the intruders to a snowmobile trail we don't want. We are now in the process of moving larger trees from other areas to this unprotected perimeter in the hope of reducing points of entry.

One day, perhaps, the only winter tracks will be those of the wild things that don't require noisy machines to propel them.

27

Birds at the Border

Christmas found us in California. In spite of a financial short-fall, we were able to pack up our ancient motor home and head west—a trip made possible by the promise of multiple assignments for San Diego Zoo's monthly publication *ZOONOOZ*. Friends Bill and Marilee Fischbeck generously offered us their boat carport for parking, complete with power and water hook-ups—and a fantastic view of the El Cajon Valley.

While we had our morning coffee inside our motor home, we watched hawks soar up thermals rising out of the valley. Black phoebes snagged flying insects just outside the door of our rig, and a flock of green parakeets, one of a number of tropical caged birds that have escaped and established small breeding colonies around the country, occasionally flew in from somewhere across the valley and landed in a large pine tree outside the Fischbecks' home. We were never able to figure out which species they were, but they were thoroughly entertaining.

Bill Fischbeck is an avid outdoorsman who has long enjoyed hiking, backpacking, and fishing. In recent years, he and Marilee have added bird watching to their interests. Every trip to southern California finds us in the field with the Fischbecks for at least one full day. Together we've been to bird-rich Newport Back Bay and Bolsa Chica State Ecological Reserve in Orange County, explored the San Diego River, Mission Bay, and Point Loma areas, and birded the Laguna Mountains. This year we planned our trip around San Diego's best-known South County hotspot—the Tijuana Slough National Wildlife Refuge, located within sight of the Mexican border.

Because our travels away from Michigan are limited to the winter months, there are southwestern birds we don't ever expect to see. Among them are birds like sulphur-bellied flycatchers and hepatic tanagers that are only found in this country during breeding season. Every year, however, a few birds that should head for the tropics after nesting take a wrong turn and end up somewhere else. Telephone and Internet hot lines have been set up to alert birders to such rarities. A tropical kingbird was one rarity reported in the San Diego about the time we arrived. This Mexican breeder occurs in a very small region in southern Arizona during the summer months and then moves south again in the fall. Once in a while one of these birds finds itself in California during the winter—to the delight of people like Jimmy and me who would otherwise never see it.

The tropical kingbird is a beautiful robin-sized bird with soft gray head, olive back, dark wings and tail, and bright yellow breast. At first glance, it looks much like a Cassin's kingbird, a close relative that occurs regularly in southern California during the winter. But closer observation reveals that the tropical kingbird has a larger bill, darker ear patch, and distinctly notched tail.

We heard about the rarity a few days before our scheduled trip to the refuge, where we planned to search for the endangered light-footed clapper rail, a life bird for our friends. But the kingbird had taken up temporary residence beside the ponds straddling a road leading to the refuge, so we stopped there first. The kingbird would be a life bird for all four of us.

Kingbirds perch on prominent snags or fence posts to hunt for insects and they are usually easy to spot. But our target bird wasn't cooperative. Four pairs of eyes searched leafless trees around the edge of the pond without success. The stop wasn't entirely fruitless; there were wintering warblers including a common yellowthroat and a black-and-white (another bird out of its range), one rufous hummingbird, a swarm of Anna's hummingbirds, northern shovelers, pied-billed grebes, and a single male ruddy duck decked out in full breeding plumage. The ruddy's blue bill looked like a child with a penchant for bright colors had painted it.

After nearly an hour searching the ponds, we decided that perhaps the bird had left the area. We agreed that after eating the lunch we had packed we would give up our search and be on our way. Then, just as we finished our sandwiches, a robin-sized bird flew in from the west and landed on a utility line nearby. It sallied out to snatch a flying insect with a sharp snap of its bill, then returned to its perch to wait for another wasp or fly. After hawking another insect, it flew to the pond and landed on a snag near the edge. Our kingbird had arrived. It was beautiful and quite possibly the only one Jimmy and I may ever see, but other avian possibilities called, so we left the kingbird and drove to the refuge.

Tijuana Slough National Wildlife Refuge is one of the best remaining estuarine habitats in southern California. Encompassing more than a thousand acres, this broad, flat coastal salt marsh has hosted nearly four hundred species of birds. One of the most important is the light-footed clapper rail, which is a permanent resident. If we had expected the kingbird to be an easy find, we were certain that the rail would be a tough one. Reclusive creatures, rails spend their lives skulking around dense wetland cover. Finding one is sometimes more a matter of luck than skill. But we were in for a surprise.

We birded the area around the refuge's visitor center first, where remnants of coastal sage scrub support wintering songbirds like sparrows, kinglets, and warblers. Half a dozen golden-crowned sparrows mixed in with a flock of white-crowned sparrows were a great discovery. It had been more than a decade since Jimmy and I had seen these small brown birds with a wide yellow stripe down the center of a black crown.

When we started down the trail into the broad saltwater marsh, the tide was well out, leaving nothing but narrow rivulets of water flowing through a vast web of depressions in the mud. The exposed muck was surrounded by an expanse of higher ground where thick wetland vegetation thrived. The *Guide to the National Wildlife Refuges* states that the best time to find the light-footed clapper rail is "during monthly winter high tides." But our experience that day suggested that the opposite might be true. Halfway to the end of the trail we stopped at a narrows, and there—in the center of the shallow stream—a light-footed clapper rail was out in the open having a bath. We were close enough to see it perfectly without the aid of spotting scope or binoculars, but it was as unconcerned about our presence as a robin in a backyard puddle. Its long, slightly drooped bill was streaked with rust, its breast glowed a rich cinnamon under the sun's rays, and its raised tail revealed white undertail coverts that looked like an old-fashioned bustle. It was the best view of a rail Jimmy and I ever had.

When we left the refuge, we birded the southern tip of San Diego Bay, where sandpipers, knots, avocets, stilts, and other shorebirds foraged along the edge while ducks, loons, and terns sought food in the center. Our species count for the day was nearly one hundred, a number we reached without even trying—supporting the *Lane Guide*'s claim that no other city in the country offers better birding than San Diego.

28

PARADISE DISAPPEARING
... BUT NOT YET LOST

At the eastern city limits of San Diego, a small condominium complex spills down the base of a chaparral-covered ridge of rugged hills. The little development looks out across a broad valley where the San Diego River winds through a riparian forest of native willows, cottonwoods, and sycamores. A quarter of a mile west, the river enters a gorge cut through the ancient volcanic ridge.

There, remains of the West Coast's oldest dam struggle to survive against the water's unrelenting flow. Originally twenty feet high and two hundred feet long, the dam was constructed by Spanish settlers in the early 1800s to provide a year-round water supply to Mission San Diego de Alcala—the first of California's twenty-two missions. The impounded water was funneled into an aqueduct and carried five miles down to the gardens, vineyards, and orchards of the mission.

Historically, southern California seasonal rains occasionally filled the gorge to as much as seventeen feet above the top of the dam. But during the last century a much larger dam upstream was built to serve the increasing water requirements for a growing population. Today the cleansing floods have been eliminated. By the time the river reaches the gorge, it is reduced to a sluggish stream. Still, it brings life to the valley as it sustains both Kumeyaay Lake upstream and the long riparian zone it passes through on its way to the sea.

Thirty years ago, I lived as a single parent in one of the condos overlooking the river valley. Both my son Jeff and I were products of the midwestern rural landscape, and we loved the home that was centered in the natural world. That was in the seventies. We believed the eventual destruction of the bucolic scene outside our front window was inevitable, and indeed the years since have ushered in massive development that continues to this day. But before we moved away, the foundation for a natural park was made from land that included the river valley and the ridge of hills. It eventually grew to encompass nearly seven thousand acres. Today, Mission Trails Regional Park is one of the largest urban parks in the country.

When we lived in the little condo, neither Jeff nor I had yet discovered the joy of watching birds. If we had, we would have been able to watch the two hundred species that occur in the park. Two are now endangered—the least Bell's vireo and the California gnatcatcher. Both nested within steps of our home. It is one of the great ironies of my life that in later years I would return to the place where my son grew up to search for the endangered gnatcatcher (the vireo, which is absent in winter, may forever remain on my wish list).

Jimmy and I went to Mission Trails early one January morning to look for the gray little bird with the black cap and tail. From a path near the visitor's center, we savored the slow awakening of a wild and wonderful place. The sun nudged its way above the horizon, bathing the narrow walls of Mission Gorge in golden rays of light. Dew glistened on tiny leaves of drought-tolerant plants and the air held a faint, savory scent of wild sage.

The morning silence was broken by the effervescent song

of a single unseen Bewick's wren, whose cheerful, persistent melody bubbled up from tangled recesses of a native shrub. Loose flocks of yellow-rumped warblers stirred under the warmth and began moving through scattered live oak trees in search of their first insect meals of the day. Overhead an Anna's hummingbird flew by in hot pursuit of an American kestrel that had gotten too close to its nest.

From the parking lot, we walked across the narrow park road, climbed a low rise, and listened. From inside a large coastal sage came the soft mewing of the gnatcatcher. At first we could only see movement deep within the bush, then gradually the movement took on a definite shape as the bird emerged to feed along the outer edges of the bush. There we got our first look at the gnatcatcher. A darker gray than the closely related black-tailed gnatcatcher, it was a hyperactive character, flicking its long tail constantly while it scrambled through branches and around leaves, rapidly removing insects from every surface. Then it darted through the air and landed in the center of another shrub where it began the process again. Captivated by the delicate beauty of the shy little bird, we kept our binoculars focused on the second bush and watched the gnatcatcher work its way back to the outside where it again fed at the surface.

Both the California gnatcatcher and the least Bell's vireo, though driven to the edge of extinction, play an important role in preserving what little is left of the natural world in their former habitat. Because of their endangered status, the presence of these little birds has either significantly altered or eliminated development plans for the few remaining riparian zones and scattered remnants of coastal sage scrub in southern California. Thus the value of the gnatcatcher and vireo reaches beyond the charm each brings to the lives of those who have discovered them.

29

BIRDING OUR WAY BACK

In 1901 a forty-mile-long irrigation canal was opened to divert water from the Colorado River to southern California's arid Imperial Valley. Three years later, the river flooded and altered its course. For the following eighteen months, millions of gallons of water pouring through the canal filled a rift in the valley known as the Salton Trough. Before the river was turned back, it created a lake thirty-five miles long and ten miles wide. The lake was called Salton Sea because of its high alkalinity, the result of the valley's extremely alkaline soils.

In spite of the salt content, Salton Sea is favored by overwintering waterfowl and other kinds of birds. The southern portion has been set aside as the Salton Sea National Wildlife Refuge, and it is a haven for the thousands of grebes, ducks, pelicans, and geese that winter there. It is also heaven for the thousands of birders who visit annually. This avian magnet was our first stop on our way home from California after camping at the Fischbecks' home. Orange County friends Malcolm and Roxane Morrison joined us.

Ponds and wetlands, created near the visitor's center to increase diversity, provide habitat for rails and herons, and dense stands of salt cedar along a network of dikes offer shelter for resident, wintering, and migrating songbirds. A hundred miles to the north, the snow-crowned San Bernardino Mountains stand serenely above the horizon, and to the east the barren ridge of the Chocolate Mountains cuts diagonally across the desert floor.

When we arrived, the sky was a pure crystalline blue, cleansed of smog and dust by a rare rain the night before. Not far from the refuge entrance a plump burrowing owl stood sentry outside the irrigation pipe that served as its burrow. The short-tailed, sandy-colored little bird was a welcome sight, another species Jimmy and I hadn't seen in years.

Inside the refuge office, we checked the log for unusual sightings and learned that someone had discovered a vermilion flycatcher. We made a note of its location and then walked along the dikes to the open water of Salton Sea where we indulged in a visual feast. Hundreds of northern pintails tilted tails up to feed and an equal number of ruddy ducks and eared grebes dived for food. Lesser numbers of mallards, cinnamon teal, and green-winged teal mingled with American wigeons. A lone Eurasian wigeon swam among them. On the opposite side of the dike, thousands of snow geese grazed in a wet meadow. And there were more northern shovelers tucked up along the muddy shoreline than we could count.

In addition to the abundance of waterfowl, there were songbirds and shorebirds, raptors and waders. A verdin—a tiny, mustard-headed songbird—teased us from the center of a salt cedar but refused to come out and provide us with a good look despite our efforts to persuade it to do so.

We spent hours birding the canals and open water at Salton Sea. On our way back to the parking lot, I caught sight of a big bird out of the corner of my eye. Though I only caught a brief glimpse of it, I immediately recognized the tawny bird with the floppy flight of a giant moth.

"Short-eared owl," I said softly.

Four pairs of binoculars were instantly focused on the golden bird as it flew over the meadow. Its flat face turned downward as it fluttered over the field looking for mice and voles. The short-eared owl flew back and forth across the open field with the slow, buoyant wing beats of its kind, and then stretched its long wings in a skyward V and dropped gently to the ground. The owl rose again shortly and continued its search, even though it carried a small rodent securely in its talons. We watched the beautiful bird for a quarter of an hour, then left it alone to hunt. This owl, only the second we'd ever seen and the first for the Morrisons, provided the ideal ending to a perfect day of birding.

From the Salton Sea, Jimmy and I went to Tucson, where we parked our RV next to my sister Judy's home. Two days after we arrived, we rose with the sun and drove to the dusty, artsy town of Patagonia. An old town with a bit of a Wild West feel, Patagonia lies in a once-verdant floodplain cradled by the Patagonia Mountains on the east and the Santa Rita range to the west. It is a place where you can spend time browsing galleries and shops or you can take your horse and ride the backcountry. But we don't own horses and we almost never shop. We were in search of a bird.

This small community is home to about fifteen hundred people, many of whom came to escape the accelerating pace that plagues much of our world. But its abundant avian population has historically attracted bird lovers from across the country and around the planet. As the popularity of bird watching grows, so do the numbers of visitors to this otherwise quiet town. While locals occasionally grouse over the crush of tourists, visitors will find it to be a peaceful place.

Sonoita Creek meanders across the western edge of town and feeds a lush riparian habitat of towering old cottonwoods and spreading willows. The rich variety of avifauna associated with this watershed inspired early residents to name the place "valley of the birds." In spite of environmental changes brought by settlers and those who came after them, the name is still appropriate.

In 1966 the Nature Conservancy purchased three hundred acres along the creek and established the Patagonia-Sonoita Creek Preserve. The preserve is now more than twice its original size and runs along roughly two miles of the stream. This wonderful property has hosted nearly three hundred species of birds. Some of them are Mexican species that spill over into our country only in the southernmost part of Arizona. These birds—including violet-crowned hummingbirds, thick-billed kingbirds, and rose-throated becards—make the preserve a place treasured by birders.

Among the species found in the preserve are four of the six towhees occurring in North America. One of them, the green-tailed, has eluded us in spite of many hours spent birding in the desert southwest. It was the hope of finding the green-tailed towhee that drove us from our morning slumber on that Sunday. We were joined for our bird hunt by Jack and Nancy Waldron, who winter in Patagonia.

After collecting the Waldrons from their RV park, we made our way to Pennsylvania Avenue and turned west. In less than a block, the pavement disappeared and the dirt road ran straight into Sonoita Creek. There was no bridge, only a sign warning drivers not to enter the creek when it is flooded. The creek is wide at this crossing and there are no markings to indicate how deep the water is, but Jimmy drove through without a second thought. Arizona was experiencing a drought.

Just beyond the crossing, we pulled off the road and parked next to a fence surrounding the home and yard of Wally and Marion Paton. Most birders who come to Patagonia begin their visit with a stop at the home of this generous couple, where large nectar feeders attract an abundance of hummingbirds throughout the year. The Patons have graciously opened their yard to all comers, and they have even put up an open-sided tent and arranged folding chairs under it to enable bird watchers to observe the comings and goings at the feeders while sitting in the shade. Violet-crowned, broad-billed, and black-chinned hummingbirds are all present from March through September. Costa's and Anna's are there throughout the year but are more common outside of the summer months. The rare plain-capped starthroat is a remote possibility in late summer. During half an hour of watching several species of these tiny flying jewels, we picked up two life birds when calliope and violet-crowned hummers showed up at the feeders. On an earlier visit, Jimmy and I picked up our first lazuli bunting at a seed feeder.

We fed the "Sugar Fund" can on our way out and left for the preserve. There we took the Railroad Trail—the remnant roadbed for an old Santa Fe line—to the Creek Trail where gigantic, gnarled cottonwoods were alive with birds. Warblers, kinglets, and bridled titmice worked their way along the bark and under leaves in search of insects and larvae. Across the creek, a house wren serenaded his lady with a sweet song and spread his tail in what we all guessed was a courtship display.

Down the path, a great blue heron eyed us warily from a weedy field outside the woods and a Say's phoebe darted after insects from a fence post in the clearing. Around a bend, we came across several small flocks of towhees. Searching each group carefully, we found only spotted and Abert's.

Farther on, a mixed flock of sparrows and juncos picked through dry leaves. Back out in the weedy field, a lone bird clung to the top of a dead stalk. I passed on the clinging bird and raised my binoculars to study the flock.

Nancy whispered from behind me, "Your towhee's on that stalk."

Too late. I caught only the olive-green tail as the bird vanished into the dead grasses, eluding me once again. Missing out on a life bird is disappointing, but never so disappointing as to spoil a day of birding no matter where we are. That's even more true of a day at Patagonia-Sonoita Creek Preserve.

30

DAWN SONG

We were home from the Southwest by the end of March. Early winds from the south had warmed the landscape, melted the snow, and carried in a couple of pleasant surprises. Among them was the return of our bluebirds—a full week early. Their arrival brought a call from our old neighbor Dave, who had lost his bluebird nestlings the summer before to a marauding raccoon. After the loss, Dave had phoned to ask if we knew how to prevent further predator destruction, and we recommended Frank Zuern's nest box. He had said that he would stop by and pick up the blueprint but hadn't gotten around to doing that before the bluebirds returned.

Bluebirds were back in his meadow at the end of February, and our old neighbor was at our door not long after we returned from the West, looking for nest box plans. After a discussion of nesting birds, national politics, and local gossip over a cup of coffee, Dave and I went for a hike on Friendship Trail. Jimmy stayed behind to finish up the taxes.

Friendship Trail, the first of what will be several similar pathways scattered around Charter Sanctuary, was punched through by seven friends the year Jimmy broke his back. The creek through the woods was too broad to jump, and on the east side of our land—beyond the woods and opposite our house—an impenetrable tangle of wild raspberries grew up the hillside. Before the trail was in, it was impossible to walk through the woods and across the east side of our property. One Sunday afternoon, seven wonderful friends—men and women who ranged in age from fifty-three to seventy-two—came and labored like slaves. For five hours these hearty souls used wheelbarrows, a chainsaw, shovels, pitchforks, and several pairs of clippers to cut, clip, chop, move saplings, haul chips, and build a footbridge, fashioning a wide walking path from a narrow track left by white-tailed deer. At the end of the day, we could walk with ease from our small fruit orchard down through the woods, across the creek, along the back of our cattail wetland, and up through the wild raspberry patch and a dense stand of pin cherries growing on the hillside across from our house.

The following September, Jeff helped build a boardwalk so that we could cross the wetland. Jimmy cut barn boards and Jeff fastened them to cedar logs. They built the boardwalk in sections and Jeff laid the sections down through the cattails. Then it was possible, for the first time since we took possession of this land, to make a complete loop around the property without leaving it.

When Dave and I left the house that balmy spring morning, we walked down to the boardwalk, and there, scurrying down the middle, was our first song sparrow of the season. Unlike Dave's bluebird, our sparrow was right on time. So were the red-winged blackbirds that had descended into the wetland the day before.

We crossed the boardwalk and hiked to the top of the hill from which we could see the boundaries of Charter Sanctuary. Other hills rolled away to the west—just a few short miles beyond them was Lake Michigan. From where Dave and I stood, we could see only four homes—two were constructed after ours, symbols of the increasing developmental pressures on farm-land in our county—and a single old barn on a distant ridge. Except for those buildings, all else was woodland, orchards, and rolling meadows.

We walked down to Friendship Trail where chickadees, stirred by the same sunny weather that had brought Dave and me out onto the trail, chirped at us from every bush and tree all the way down the hill. When we reached the back of the wetland, I pointed out the site where the woodcock hen had nested the previous year.

"Her mate is already peenting in our meadow," I said. "Like our bluebirds, he's a week early, but he's already out in the meadow peenting to establish his territory. The hens probably haven't gotten back yet."

As we left the woods and hiked back to the house, Dave expressed the kind of astonishment we had felt when we first saw the property as a whole. Like us, he knew its perimeter well. Also like us, he had no idea how diverse the interior is.

"You two certainly picked the right place for what you're doing. This property is fantastic," he said. "I can't believe how many different habitats are tucked inside; there are all kinds of little surprises here. You and Jimmy surely did find the perfect spot for your efforts."

The following day our turkey hen returned and took up her old tricks. The summer before, this big bird left her nest each afternoon to steal sunflower seeds from under our feeder. She would feed for an hour or so and then stroll casually back up our drive. If we opened the front door while she was feeding, she would trot down the slope away from the house, through a narrow woods, and across a small stream that runs behind the barn. A strip of trees and shrubs along the stream has a little opening just east of the barn. The bird would make her way to that opening and stand there, peering back at us through the branches, waiting for the coast to clear so she could return to her snack.

Although I believe that anthropomorphizing tends to diminish wild creatures, when this long-legged bird craned her long neck around the trees to check on us, she looked so like a

human that it was impossible not to make that comparison. It was clear by her actions that turkeys don't deserve the reputation they hold for being stupid. This bird knew exactly what she wanted and she had figured out precisely how to get it.

After the turkey hen came back, our male phoebe returned and began singing from the top branches of the reincarnated maple tree we call Lazarus. Two days later, winter returned and held the land in its frigid fingers. A bitter wind bore down from the north and the phoebe disappeared. The third day dawned bright and sunny, if not warm, and the plump gray-and-white bird returned to sing and pump his tail from the top of the maple. That same morning a second phoebe, a female, arrived to check out the nest ledge. She carefully studied the home her prospective mate had selected. Satisfied that it would serve her needs, she darted out to snatch an insect and returned to the ledge.

It was a delight to have them back. But then the cold deepened and both birds were gone. They stayed away for more than a week, and I fretted about them during their absence. How on earth would these plump little flycatchers survive subfreezing temperatures? Kenn Kaufman says in his wonderful work *Lives of North American Birds* that phoebes eat berries and other fruits when insects aren't available, but there was no fruit this time of year.

When the weather moderated, only the male came back to the barn. We'd never know what had happened to the hen, and where the male had been and what had he survived on.

After the phoebe returned, the first killdeer of the year began calling from the south side of our meadow, and an eastern meadowlark added his plaintive melody to the growing chorus of avian voices drifting up from the land. While the full force of spring migration was still two months away, we were in that preseason period when breeding birds trickle in to stake claims on territory they wouldn't even use until May or June. These annual early birds are a little like an elaborate tray of hor's d'oeuvres presented prior to an elegant gourmet dinner— an enticing sample of the wonderful things to come.

Tree swallows and barn swallows were followed by eastern kingbirds. Then a male house wren arrived and laid claim to nest boxes Jimmy had put up for him in the pin cherries. By the end of May as many as fifty different species settled on this little piece of land to nest, each adding its unique sound to the rich layers of song. Then, every morning for three weeks, these birds collectively lifted their voices with the rising sun and made a joyful noise more glorious than anything Beethoven or Bach ever dreamed of. It's a phenomenon I didn't know at all until we moved here.

It is called the dawn song.

Now I wait for it each year as eagerly as a kid waits for Christmas.

31

THE NUTS AND BOLTS OF CHARTER SANCTUARY

We knew when we established our sanctuary that in the vast scheme of things, forty-seven acres is less than the proverbial drop in a bucket of what is needed to assist the birds that need help. In order to increase the impact of our purchase, I planned to conduct classes here to help others who care about birds improve the habitat in their own yards. The spring after we moved into our home, the first group of fifteen bird-loving souls came to find out how to do that. There has been a steady stream of class participants every year since.

We've also had hundreds of other visitors of all ages. School kids have come here—so have women's clubs and Audubon groups. Our B&B is popular because people want to share in our experience, and my classes have been well received, even though I am by no means a trained teacher.

Class participants and some visitors often ask what kind of seeds they should use to attract more birds. My answer is always the same: While offering food will bring some species in for closer observation, we actually attract birds to our yards by providing them with the habitat they need.

The process of creating a backyard sanctuary is simple, it seems to me. First, preserve all dead trees that do not threaten life or limb. These will provide nest sites for woodpeckers, owls, chickadees, titmice, nuthatches, and other species—even in urban settings.

Then keep your pet cats indoors. Domestic and feral cats kill an estimated seven hundred million birds a year in this country alone. Contrary to popular belief, putting bells on cats appears to have little effect on their ability to kill birds, research has shown. Many people are under the impression that not allowing pet cats to roam is inhumane. The opposite may actually be true; keeping them indoors will not only protect songbirds from predation, it will protect the animals themselves from disease, attack, and injury. Furthermore, our experience, and that of friends and relatives, has shown that cats that have never been allowed access to the outdoors suffer no emotional trauma. Our two cats have never been out of doors, but they are happy, healthy, loving creatures.

Once you have made your yard safe for avian visitors, create habitat that invites them in. You can do that by following Tom Ford's advice: get rid of your lawnmower and then stuff as many native trees, grasses, and flowers as you can into the area you want to develop. For inspiration, I recommend Sara Stein's informative and delightfully readable book *Noah's Garden* in which she traces her own personal journey from backyard gardener to steward of ten acres in New York. In her book, Stein instructs all of us on how to replace high-maintenance, sterile lawns with attractive, easy-care native plantings. She also writes that if each of us returned large portions of our lots to native plantings, much of suburbia would be restored and returned to birds, butterflies, mammals, and other creatures that were the original inhabitants. Imagine backyards in every neighborhood in the East hosting catbirds and cardinals and every one in the Southwest supporting tiny, beautiful verdins and gregarious, entertaining cactus wrens.

For those who want more detailed examples of developing habitat, there are many books on the subject. The National Audubon Society's *The Bird Garden* by Stephen W. Kress is an excellent first choice; it includes not only regional suggestions but also helpful photos and drawings, as well as some of the species attracted to particular plantings.

In our yard, Jimmy and I followed Stein's example in the front of our home, which after the house was built was nothing more than weeds, cut occasionally to allow us to get around outdoors without wading through waist-deep vegetation. It was functional, but not very attractive—either to us or to the flocks of birds that otherwise found our land ideal for their needs. The rough lawn was nearly devoid of birds.

We developed habitat that would welcome friends, both footed and feathered. We began by digging up several small northern white cedar trees from here and there around our property and planting them in tight clusters right up against the house. Cedars are especially good for birds because they provide close cover throughout the year. Some birds, including waxwings and pine siskins, eat the fruit, while many other species benefit from the variety of insects drawn to this attractive and hardy native tree. While cedar plantings may have to be protected from deer browse in some parts of the country with fencing or hardware cloth, they are well worth the trouble such protection might entail because they provide food and cover for so many species, especially during migration.

Next we laid down a wide curving path of cedar chips the power company left when it opened the route for a new line. The path leads from the driveway to the entry, and it branches off down to the south side—the trail the turkey hen follows when she feels the need to hide while she is filching seed. After the path was laid down, we added what I call an "instant thicket" up against the house using red osier dogwood, serviceberries, and highbush cranberries dug up from the hillside across the creek. It took just over a week to plant this "thicket." Our song sparrows didn't wait for us to finish; they began to kick around under the shrubs every time the shovels went back into the shed.

As soon as we finished our plantings, Jimmy stuck a feeder pole in the ground about four feet from the window next to my desk and hung a seed feeder and a nectar feeder on it. I filled a ceramic planter saucer with water and put it on the ground near the feeders. It took about three days for the birds to make use of the makeshift birdbath, but they discovered the feeders immediately. The song sparrows were first, followed rapidly by the hummingbirds. Because we finished our project during the early days of hummingbird migration, the nectar tube was emptied nearly every day. Hummers were followed by chickadees and by purple finches and rose-breasted grosbeaks.

Since then the front of our home has become a haven for a variety of foraging sparrows, grosbeaks, and finches. Catbirds love it. This small area—less than four hundred square feet—is alive with birds. It serves as an example for visitors who can see how easy it would be to attract more birds to their own yards.

So Charter Sanctuary is more than a place for birds to live. It is also a place for birders to learn, even if the teacher is far more student than sage.

32

BIRDS ARE AMAZING

One evening when Tom Ford was dining with us, we were talking about the collective marvels of avifauna.

"Birds are simply..." I started and then stopped. I couldn't find an adjective that adequately described them.

"They are amazing," Tom said quietly.

"They are amazing," I agreed.

In our overstimulated world of shoot-'em-up, highly sexed films and literature, words sometimes lose their value. *Webster's New International Dictionary, Second Edition* (subsequent editions have sacrificed the vigor of our language) defines *amazing* thusly: "To overwhelm with bewildered wonder..."

There is no question that I am overwhelmed with bewildered wonder at the bird life around us. I am certainly not alone; increasing numbers of people from around the world are similarly affected. What is it about birds that so intrigues us? They are the most widespread vertebrates on the planet, and to some of us, they are the most beautiful and fascinating of all nature's creatures. Who would fail to be moved by the grace and beauty of a pair of cranes engaged in an exuberant courtship dance? It is not, however, simply their glorious feathered finery or the beauty of their movement that woos us. Nature provides countless examples of beauty. And I don't think it's even because they can defy gravity and fly, even though our own species has envied that unique ability since the time of early man.

The reason for our fascination with birds is as complicated as they are. For many people, it may begin with the realization that birds are all around us, yet we don't see them until our eyes are opened by some special experience. For me, it was a bufflehead diving for food in San Diego Bay that caught my attention and opened up the world of birds. For Jeff, it was a pileated woodpecker hopping along the trail when the two of us were hiking in an Idaho forest.

When Jeff first got into the business of birding, he was asked to survey the kinds of birds on one of the many golf courses in the desert city of Tucson, Arizona. The environmental company he worked for wanted to document which species frequented the artificial, chemically maintained habitat there. He approached the manager of the course for permission to carry out the survey, and the man said, "Birds? I've been here for years and haven't seen a single bird yet. You can do your study if you like, but I can assure you that we don't have any birds here."

I grew up in southern Illinois farming country. Our home was on a quarter-mile-long unpaved drive with two other houses. A fallow field lay across the road and a large woodland bordered one side of our lot. My siblings and I spent many hours in that field and woodlot. But like the golf course manager in Tucson, if someone had asked any of us what kind of birds were in those woods, we likely would all have answered, "There are no birds here."

If the man in the desert or the kids romping in the Illinois woodland had known anything about birds, they would have known that birds had to be both on the golf course and in our field and woods. There are roughly ten thousand avian species on earth, and they are found virtually everywhere—at sea as well as on land, from the extreme latitudes of the Arctic to the harsh climes of Antarctica.

They are, moreover, much more complex than they first appear to be, and there are extraordinary differences between one species and another. There are birds, like chickadees, whose social structures are as complex as that of many mammals. Communication is complicated, both within a species and, when it happens, across species. A cry of alarm from one bird at a feeder will be immediately understood by every other bird at the feeder and will send the lot of them in a frantic search for cover. But a bird that nests in dense colonies, like the northern gannet, and recognizes the sounds made by its mate or young by vocalization does not recognize a particular neighboring pair or chick by the same kind of vocalization.

Ostriches have lost the ability to fly, while roadrunners can fly but prefer to run from danger. On the opposite end of the spectrum, marathon fliers such as arctic terns make a twenty-five-thousand-mile round-trip migration between breeding and wintering grounds every year of their lives.

Some birds, including those of the albatross family, spend their entire lives at sea, coming to land just long enough to nest and raise their young. Others live in environments that seem too hostile to support birds. The tiny elf owl, which is smaller than an eastern bluebird, often makes its home in the shimmering summer heat of the desert Southwest.

There are opportunistic and adaptive species, like the European starling, that can nest almost anywhere. But other species are so highly specialized that when their habitat is destroyed, they disappear entirely. If the young jack pine stands around Grayling, Michigan, were not managed on their behalf, the rare Kirtland's warbler would likely be extinct by now.

A few species have developed behaviors more unbelievable than anything Disney could dream up. The American dipper, a small gray bird found only along fast-running streams in the mountains of the North American West, is one such character. Nicknamed the water ouzel for its habit of feeding on insect larva at the bottom of streams, the dipper will sometimes dive from a boulder to the bottom of a twenty-foot-deep pool. When it's ready to move from one place to another, this astonishing little bird simply flies straight up out of the water like a miniature Polaris missile and then cruises over the surface to a new feeding place. The dipper, which weighs just over an ounce, can forage in water too deep and fast flowing for humans to stand in.

Birds are not only far more intelligent than we once realized, many are extremely inquisitive. Some years ago, keepers at the San Diego Zoo were stunned upon entering the bird yard one morning to find that the kitchen had been completely ransacked during the night. Food was everywhere, equipment was overturned, feed bags were ripped open and their contents were scattered across the floor. The culprit, they were surprised to learn, was a kea, a bird whose enclosure backed up to the building housing the bird yard. Keas are intensely curious and are infamous in the wild for being irrepressibly mischievous. In the mountains of New Zealand where they occur, skiers sometimes return from a day on the slopes to find their cars partially dismantled by these inquisitive creatures. The kea in the bird yard was just following its natural inclination; using its strong bill, the kea rattled the door of its cage until the slide latch moved enough for it to open the door. It then spent the night entertaining itself by undoing everything in the kitchen.

There are other examples of avian play: Australian galahs slide down the guy wires of television towers, and Anna's hummingbirds have been seen riding down streams of water from garden hoses. Once, while birding with friends Bill and Marilee Fischbeck in southern California's Laguna Mountains, a small flock of ravens entertained themselves—and us—by tumbling down a wind draft along a steep slope. When the birds reached the bottom of the slope, they flew back to the top to begin again. In Iceland common eiders have been observed shooting rapids in much the way our ravens rode down the wind current. Upon reaching the bottom, these large sea ducks dashed back to the top of the rapids and rode down again.

Alexander Skutch, a well-known field ornithologist who has spent his long life in the field, maintained that avian play was proof of bird intelligence. "Only conscious beings are capable of enjoyment," he wrote. Play not only promotes development in young, it also contributes to the learning process for all individuals.

Many species use tools. Green jays in Texas and woodpecker finches on the Galapagos Islands extract insects and larva deeply embedded in tree bark with the aid of twigs or cactus spines. Egyptian vultures hurl stones at the hard shells of ostrich eggs to crack them, and bristle-thighed curlews open albatross eggs with pieces of coral. Indian tailorbirds stitch leaves together with cobwebs to create cocoonlike nests, and Japanese green herons and Kenyan pied kingfishers have actually learned to fish with bait. The herons, for example, toss captured insects or bits of rubbish on the water to lure fish.

When Jimmy and I once called on B&B owner Linda Metz in the tiny Arizona town of Arivaca, she introduced us to Tyler, her blue-and-gold macaw. She placed Tyler on her shoulder while we chatted. Tyler walked up Linda's arm where he stopped on her shoulder to rub her head with his own before stretching around to her face to nibble her cheek gently with his large, powerful beak. Then he walked back down his mistress's arm toward his perch. He stood on her wrist for a moment, bobbing his head up and down, then leaned forward and said, "Help!" in a course, gravely voice.

Tyler's wings were clipped so that he couldn't fly, and his place on Linda's arm was too far away from the perch for him to simply step up on it. With a smile, his mistress moved her arm closer to the wooden dowel and the bird immediately hopped on it. Until recently, experts would have insisted that Tyler had no idea what he was saying, holding firmly to the view that although parrots could mimic our own speech, they had absolutely no idea what the words meant. But that view is changing; now many agree that this great parrot knew exactly what he was saying.

There are birds that have learned to count and to recognize as many as eight colors, and they can identify and request by name up to forty individual objects. In the wild, some birds build fantastic, elaborate structures that they decorate with entirely nonessential lichens, feathers, flowers, and—in the case of one Australian bowerbird—sun-bleached bones and shells. Satin bowerbirds paint the inside walls of their bowers with berry pulp by using wads of fibrous bark for sponges.

Songbird nestlings and fledglings must be taught the precise and complicated melodies necessary for courtship; this fundamental skill is not inherent. Many flocking species have complex social systems that, intuition tells us, require at least some level of intelligence.

One of the most astonishing examples of bird intelligence involves a great tit that lived in the English country garden of a woman by the name of Len Howard. Howard's devotion to avifauna was so deep that she opened her home to the birds around her. During the nesting season, the tit would come into Howard's bedroom through an open window and awaken her whenever a roving magpie threatened its eggs or nestlings. The tit would issue a cry of alarm, flying between the bed and the window, until Howard roused herself and went outside to chase the magpie off with a stick. The tit had to have learned, in much the way that our beggar black-capped chickadee has, that this woman not only meant it no harm, but was actually a friend.

It's no wonder that birds have captured our collective interest and imagination. Watching them is a satisfying way to spend time for everyone, from the backyard enthusiast who daily greets a cardinal at the feeder to the serious birder who slogs tirelessly through the Amazon River Basin in search of a glimpse of the rare rufous potoo.

Jeff's survey on the Arizona golf course is proof that birds are all around us, but we don't see them until we look. On a single day in October he identified more than sixty species of birds, including the elegant peregrine falcon.

Today, a growing number of people are discovering for the first time these wonderful creatures that have been before their eyes all along.

33

LEGACY

In February 1986, we were camped in a trailer on the shell reef at Goose Island State Park in Texas. Our trailer was backed up to Aransas Bay. At dawn the morning after we arrived, Jimmy called me from the living room area of our little rig.

"There's a family of whoopers out here."

I awoke immediately from a deep sleep and bounded to the back of the trailer. Sure enough, less than thirty feet away, three whooping cranes were picking through the oysters in search of food. It was the first time on record these magnificent and highly endangered birds had visited the park. Six years later we were back at the park. So were the whoopers. That year we camped on the opposite end of the island—and that year the whoopers were on the opposite end as well.

The first time we were blessed with a visit by a whooping crane family, we felt like we'd experienced a remarkable event. The second time was more like a miracle. Jimmy and I may be the only people on the planet—except for park personnel—who were at Goose Island for both of these visits—the only two on record.

One day after we had sold our Michigan cottage on the water and had no idea of where we were going to live until we found land for a sanctuary, Mary Lou Griffin said to me, "I think God is watching out for you." Mary Lou is a woman of strong faith who believes that God is intricately involved in every single transaction of each of our lives. I am still trying to figure out what I believe about God. But I remembered the whooping cranes and thought to myself that she might just be right.

"If that is true," I said to her, "it is because I'm drawn to His most astonishing creation—the birds." The situation brought to mind a conversation I'd had with a writer on a train. "I think the Creator has a special relationship with birds," he said.

My determination to help the birds goes beyond a desire to do something positive with my life. It is something I must do. It is like a calling; without it my soul would wither just as surely as my body would without food. The place we now share with these remarkable beings, these forty-seven acres, has provided my life with a meaning it previously lacked. It has been a blessing beyond measure.

The year after we moved into our home on the sanctuary, we set aside the first thirteen acres under a permanent conservation easement with the Leelanau Conservancy. The easement mandates that these acres must be forever managed for the benefit of songbirds, under guidelines that we established. While the title to the property remains in our hands, no one may use it without our express permission, and no one can ever develop it in any way, either during or after our lifetimes. Once we are gone, the entire sanctuary—lock, stock, and buildings—will go to the Conservancy.

When we bought the property, we stood at the top of the hill and said that we would manage it for the birds and then leave it to them upon our death. For me, the effect of the easement was that we were able to grant this land to our beloved birds before we die and still enjoy the effect of our legacy.

After the easement was in place, a reporter from a local television station called to to arrange an interview. While I was waiting for him to arrive, I watched a common yellowthroat fledgling beg for food from its perch on a willow branch. The young bird's male parent quickly answered the call. The reporter missed the little drama, but the image of the beautiful warbler feeding its offspring was fresh in my mind when he asked how I felt about this land.

"All I can tell you is this, " I said, "If heaven is anything like this place, I am going to have to change my ways."

APPENDICES

How You Can Help

- Keep cats indoors. Recent studies show that domestic and feral cats kill more than seven hundred million birds every year in the United States alone. That is an unacceptable number.

- Share your yard with birds and other wildlife. Gradually replace ornamental plants with groupings of native trees and shrubs around the perimeter. Then plant native grasses and wildflowers along the edge of those trees and shrubs. Reduce the mowed area by 50 percent or more. Provide a birdbath, which should be cleaned daily with a scrub brush and refilled with fresh water.

- Do not cut dead trees unless they threaten life, limb, or buildings. Cavity nesters like woodpeckers, owls, nuthatches, titmice, chickadees, several ducks, and two North American warblers depend on dead and dying trees for nest sites.

- Use squirrelproof feeders. If you feed birds, try not to feed squirrels and other rodents. The more food available to them, the more there will be.

- Use windows with screens outside. If you are planning a new home, avoid plate glass windows. Using windows with screens helps to protect birds from window crashes. That is especially true if you are building in a wooded area.

- Don't entrap your songbirds. Take feeders down if a bird-eating hawk (sharp-shinned, Cooper's, goshawk) takes up residence in your yard. Keep them down until your regular feeder visitors disperse and the hawk leaves.

- Switch to shade-grown coffee. If you are a coffee drinker, pay a little more for coffee grown under tropical canopies. Sun coffee plantations destroy forest canopies that provide winter habitat for many birds. By using coffees that do not come from sun plantations, you can help preserve that habitat. If your local retailers and specialty stores do not carry a brand of shade-grown coffee, ask that they do. Following are several web sites that offer information about this issue and list some brands:

> Café Canopy
> www.shade-coffee.com
>
> *Shade-coffee developed in cooperation with the Smithsonian Migratory Bird Center.*
>
> Conservation International
> www.conservation.org/coffee/the_program.htm
>
> *Research and conservation advocate organization. They list one or two brands.*
>
> Equal Exchange
> www.equalexchange.com
>
> *Important importer and vendor of fair trade coffees.*
>
> Montana Coffee Traders
> www.coffeetraders.com/menu.html
>
> *Roasters working in cooperation with the Northwest Shade Coffee Campaign.*
>
> Smithsonian Migratory Bird Center
> www.si.edu/smbc/coffee.htm
>
> *Research organization that has developed a set of bird-compatible coffee farming criteria. See their Coffee Corner.*

Thanksgiving Coffee Co.
www.songbirdcoffee.com

Vendor of Song Bird Coffee, in association with the ABA.

The Nature Conservancy's "Save the Rainforest" Site
www.therainforestsite.com

At this site you can click on a button that will provide donations of rainforest land by the site's sponsors. Also information on shade-grown coffee.

• Join wildlife and nature organizations:

Land Trust Alliance
1331 H St NW, Suite 400, Washington, DC 20005
Phone 202-638-4725; Fax 202-638-4730
Web site: www.lta.org

Contact the Land Trust Alliance and find out if one of the more than 1,200 local land trusts and conservancies is in your area. If there is, join it and become involved in its efforts.

National Audubon Society
700 Broadway, New York, NY 10003
Phone: 212-979-3000
Web site: www.audubon.org

A national organization dedicated to conserving and restoring natural ecosystems, focusing on birds and biological diversity.

The Nature Conservancy
4245 Fairfax Drive, Arlington, VA 22203
Phone: 703-841-5300
Web site: www.tnc.org

This international organization preserves plant, animal, and natural communities by protecting the lands and waters on which they depend. The Nature Conservancy has protected more than 11 million acres in the U.S. and nearly 60 million in Canada, Latin America, the Caribbean, Asia, and the Pacific.

National Wildlife Federation
8925 Leesburg Pike, Vienna, VA 22184
Web site: www.nwf.org

The mission of the National Wildlife Federation is to educate, inspire and assist individuals and organizations of diverse cultures to conserve wildlife and other natural resources and to protect the Earth's environment in order to achieve a peaceful, equitable, and sustainable future.

The Wilderness Society
1615 M St, NW, Washington, DC 20036
Phone: 800-843-9453
Web site: www.wilderness.org

The Wilderness Society is dedicated to protecting America's wild lands through public education and advocacy.

American Bird Conservancy
1250 24th Street, NW, Suite 400 Washington, DC 20037
Phone: 202-778-9666; Fax: 202-778-9778
Web site: www.abcbirds.org

Dedicated to building coalitions of conservationists, scientists, and members of the general public to tackle key bird priorities using the best resources available.

Ducks Unlimited, Inc.
One Waterfowl Way, Memphis, Tennessee, 38120
Phone: 800-45DUCKS
Web site: www.ducks.org

Even if you aren't a hunter—indeed, even if you do not believe in hunting—this organization is worth joining for its sheer effectiveness in protecting critical wetland and upland habitat. Since 1937, efforts by Ducks Unlimited, Inc. have resulted in protection, enhancement, or restoration of a total of 9,442,471 acres across North America. While those acres were set aside to provide habitat for waterfowl, they have also provided habitat for many species of songbirds, shorebirds, herons, and others both during migration and the nesting season.

Trout Unlimited
1500 Wilson Boulevard; Suite 310 Arlington, VA 22209-2404
Phone: 703-522-0200 Fax: 703-284-9400 Join or Renew Toll-free: 800-834-2419
Web site: www.tu.org

Trout Unlimited has protected and restored thousands of acres of North America's watersheds for the benefit of trout and salmon fisheries. Protecting watersheds is helpful to other kinds of wildlife, including birds.

Further Reading

Able, Kenneth P., ed. 1999. *Gatherings of Angels: Migrating Birds and Their Ecology*. Ithaca, NY: Comstock Books.

> A fascinating look at the biannual transcontinental movements of birds—an absolute must for those who are spellbound by the magic of migration.

Askins, Robert A. 2000. *Restoring North America's Birds: Lessons from Landscape Ecology*. New Haven, Conn.: Yale University Press.

> Zoologist Robert Askins writes about the decline of North American songbirds, examines which habitats are involved, and explores ways to measure the health of those habitats. An essential work for those involved with conservation efforts.

Conniff, Richard. 2000. "So Tiny, So Sweet...So Mean." *Smithsonian*, Vol. 31, No.6.

> Examines the incredible lives of hummingbirds. Writer Conniff says, "People...think they're little fairies. (However) We're probably lucky these things aren't the size of ravens, or it would not be safe to walk in the woods."

Kress, Stephen W. 1985. *The Audubon Society Guide to Attracting Birds*. New York: Charles Scribner's Sons.

_____ . 1995. *The Bird Garden*. New York: DK Publishing.

> Both of Kress's books are helpful for creating backyard habitat.

Line, Les. 1993. "The Silence of the Songbirds." *National Geographic*, Vol. 183 No. 6:68-91.

> While this article was written several years ago, it provides impressive documentation of scope and causes of songbird decline.

Stein, Sara. 1993. *Noah's Garden: Restoring the Ecology of Our Own Backyards*. Boston: Houghton Mifflin.

> Engaging account of one woman's journey from formal gardener to passionate proponent of restoring native habitats in backyards across suburbia.

_____ . 1997. *Planting Noah's Garden: Further Adventures in Backyard Ecology*. New York: Houghton Mifflin.

> Sequel to above includes considerable how-to information.

Williams, Ted. 1999. "Management by Majority," *Audubon*, Vol.100, No. 3: 40-49.

> *Audubon* magazine's editor-at-large Ted Williams documents the effects of ballot initiatives that prohibit wildlife experts from managing problem species. These prohibitions can have a devastating effect on endangered species like the Great Lakes piping plover.

Bibliography

Bent, Arthur Cleveland, ed.. 1958. *Life Histories of North American Blackbirds, Orioles, Tanagers, and Allies*. Washington, D.C.: Smithsonian Institution.

———. 1942. *Life Histories of North American Flycatchers, Larks, Swallows, and Their Allies*. Washington, D.C.: Smithsonian Institution.

Brewer, Richard, Gail A. McPeek, Raymond J. Adams, Jr. 1991. *The Atlas of Breeding Birds of Michigan*. East Lansing: Michigan State University Press.

Dunne, Pete, David Sibley, Clay Sutton. 1988. *Hawks in Flight: The Flight Identification of North American Migrant Raptors*. Boston: Houghton Mifflin.

Erlich, Paul R., David S. Dobkin, Darryl Wheye. 1988. *The Birder's Handbook: A Field Guide to the Natural History of North American Birds*. New York: Simon & Schuster.

Gill, Frank B. 1994. *Ornithology*. New York: W. H. Freeman and Company.

Granlund, James [et al.]. Gail A. McPeek, ed. 1994. *The Birds of Michigan*. Bloomington, Ind: Indiana University Press.

Holt, Harold R. 1993. *A Birder's Guide to the Texas Coast*. Rev. from original text by James A. Lane. 4th ed. Colorado Springs, Colo.: American Birding Association.

_____ . 1992. *A Birder's Guide to the Rio Grande Valley of Texas.* Colorado Springs, Colo. : American Birding Association.

_____ . 1990. *A Birder's Guide to Southern California.* Colorado Springs, Colo.: American Birding Association.

Leahy, Christopher W. 1984. *The Birdwatcher's Companion: An Encyclopedic Handbook of North American Birdlife.* New York: Bonanza Books.

Line, Les. 1993. "The Silence of the Songbirds." *National Geographic,* Vol. 183, No. 6:68-91.

Kaufman, Kenn. 1996. *Lives of North American Birds.* Boston: Houghton Mifflin Co.

Kerlinger, Paul. 1995. *How Birds Migrate.* Mechanicsburg, Pa.: Stackpole Books.

Page, Jake and Eugene S. Morton. 1989. *Lords of the Air: The Smithsonian Book of Birds.* New York: Orion Books.

Perrins, Christopher M., consultant-in-chief. 1990. *The Illustrated Encyclopedia of Birds: The Definitive Reference to Birds of the World.* New York: Prentice Hall Press.

Riley, Laura and William. 1992. *Guide to the National Wildlife Refuges.* New York: MacMillan

Skutch, Alexander F. 1996. *The Minds of Birds.* College Station: Texas A&M University Press.

Taylor, Richard Cachor. 1995. *A Birder's Guide to Southeastern Arizona.* Colorado Springs, Colo.: American Birding Association.

Terres, John K. 1991. *The Audubon Society Encyclopedia of North American Birds.* New York: Wings Books.